# Praise for *The Super*

D1168846

"With wit, wisdom, and tell-all honesty, Becky reminds us that supermoms don't wear capes; they simply cling to Jesus."
—Alicia Bruxvoort, member of the Proverbs 31 writing team

"With disarming humor, transparency, and raw honesty, Becky Kopitzke makes it safe for moms to take off their capes and rest in God's provision and blessing in their sincere, passionate, and imperfect mothering."
—Melinda Means, speaker and coauthor of *Mothering from Scratch*

"*The SuperMom Myth* shatters the urban legend of the mom who has it all together."
—Kathy Helgemo, speaker and coauthor of *Mothering from Scratch*

"[*The SuperMom Myth* is] essential for every mom who has ever doubted herself. Moms, run, don't walk to snag this handbook for fighting for your sanity!"
—Lisa-Jo Baker, author of *Surprised by Motherhood* and community manager for (in)courage

"Much like Becky, I got sucked into thinking that busyness, worry, self-neglect, and exhaustion (to name a few) were all on the road to being a Supermom. She does a profound job unpacking the 8 dirty villains and then providing biblical solutions. Our homes were designed for so much more."
—Courtney DeFeo, author of *In This House, We Will Giggle* and creator of *Lil Light O' Mine*

"*The SuperMom Myth* is a practical, fun, and refreshing read for every mom!"
—Ruth Schwenk, founder of TheBetterMom.com and coauthor of *Hoodwinked: Ten Myths Moms Believe and Why We All Need to Knock It Off*

"Becky Kopitzke's gentle answers reveal biblical truths and fresh insights that every mom needs to hear. She points us all to the only Superhero who is infallible, reminding us that, by ourselves, cape or not, we can't save the day. I'll gladly serve as faithful sidekick to the One who can."
—Kelly O'Dell Stanley, author of *Praying Upside Down: A Creative Prayer Experience to Transform Your Time with God*

"Becky writes about biblical truths that are timeless, leaving us life lessons discovered in parenting that can be invaluable through the coming years."
—Judy Episcopo, international speaker and women's ministry director, Appleton Alliance Church

"With discussion questions for each chapter, *The SuperMom Myth* is definitely a MUST READ and is a great resource for moms and small groups alike."
—Stephanie Shott, author of *The Making of a Mom* and founder of The MOM Initiative

Becky Kopitzke

# THE *Super* MOM MYTH

## CONQUERING THE **DIRTY VILLAINS** OF MOTHERHOOD

SHILOH RUN PRESS
An Imprint of Barbour Publishing, Inc.

© 2015 by Becky Kopitzke

Print ISBN 978-1-63409-524-2

eBook Editions:
Adobe Digital Edition (.epub) 978-1-63409-647-8
Kindle and MobiPocket Edition (.prc) 978-1-63409-648-5

All rights reserved. No part of this publication may be reproduced or transmitted for commercial purposes, except for brief quotations in printed reviews, without written permission of the publisher.

Churches and other noncommercial interests may reproduce portions of this book without the express written permission of Barbour Publishing, provided that the text does not exceed 500 words or 5 percent of the entire book, whichever is less, and that the text is not material quoted from another publisher. When reproducing text from this book, include the following credit line: "From *The SuperMom Myth* by Becky Kopitzke, published by Barbour Publishing, Inc. Used by permission."

All scripture quotations, unless otherwise indicated, are taken from the HOLY BIBLE, NEW INTERNATIONAL VERSION®. NIV®. Copyright © 1973, 1978, 1984, 2011 by Biblica, Inc.™ Used by permission. All rights reserved worldwide.

Scripture quotations marked NKJV are taken from the New King James Version®. Copyright © 1982 by Thomas Nelson, Inc. Used by permission. All rights reserved.

Scripture quotations marked NLT are taken from the *Holy Bible*, New Living Translation copyright© 1996, 2004, 2007 by Tyndale House Foundation. Used by permission of Tyndale House Publishers, Inc. Carol Stream, Illinois 60188. All rights reserved.

Scripture quotations marked MSG are from *THE MESSAGE*. Copyright © by Eugene H. Peterson 1993, 1994, 1995, 1996, 2000, 2001, 2002. Used by permission of NavPress Publishing Group.

Scripture quotations marked KJV are taken from the King James Version of the Bible.

Scripture quotations marked TLB are taken from The Living Bible © 1971 by Tyndale House Foundation. Used by permission of Tyndale House Publishers, Inc. Wheaton, Illinois 60189. All rights reserved.

Scripture quotations marked NIRV are taken from the Holy Bible, NEW INTERNATIONAL READER'S VERSION®. Copyright © 1996, 1998 Biblica. All rights reserved throughout the world. Used by permission of Biblica.

Scripture quotations marked NASB are taken from the New American Standard Bible, © 1960, 1962, 1963, 1968, 1971, 1972, 1973, 1975, 1977, 1995 by The Lockman Foundation. Used by permission.

Scripture quotations marked NASB are taken from the New American Standard Bible, © 1960, 1962, 1963, 1968, 1971, 1972, 1973, 1975, 1977, 1995 by The Lockman Foundation. Used by permission.

Scripture quotations marked ESV are from The Holy Bible, English Standard Version®, copyright © 2001 by Crossway Bibles, a publishing ministry of Good News Publishers. Used by permission. All rights reserved.

Scripture quotations marked AMP are taken from the Amplified® Bible, © 1954, 1958, 1962, 1964, 1965, 1987

Published in association with The Blythe Daniel Agency, Inc., P.O. Box 64197, Colorado Springs, CO 80962.

Published by Shiloh Run Press, an imprint of Barbour Publishing, Inc., P.O. Box 719, Uhrichsville, Ohio 44683, www.shilohrunpress.com

*Our mission is to publish and distribute inspirational products offering exceptional value and biblical encouragement to the masses.*

Member of the
Evangelical Christian
Publishers Association

Printed in the United States of America.

# CONTENTS

*Introduction:* The Mom of My Daydreams . . . . . . . . . . . . . . . . 7

*Chapter 1:* Who Are These Little People
(and How Do I Send Them Back)? . . . . . . . . . . . . . . . . . . . . 11

*Chapter 2:* The Grouch on the Couch . . . . . . . . . . . . . . . . . . 27

*Chapter 3:* Worry Much? . . . . . . . . . . . . . . . . . . . . . . . . . . . 43

*Chapter 4:* But the Neighbors Are Doing It . . . . . . . . . . . . . . 59

*Chapter 5:* Just a Minute! . . . . . . . . . . . . . . . . . . . . . . . . . . . 77

*Chapter 6:* Am I the Maid Around Here? . . . . . . . . . . . . . . . 95

*Chapter 7:* Attack of the Zombie Mommy . . . . . . . . . . . . . 113

*Chapter 8:* Not Tonight, Dear . . . . . . . . . . . . . . . . . . . . . . . 127

*Chapter 9:* Martyr Mom Ain't No Good Guy . . . . . . . . . . . 145

*Chapter 10:* Will the Real Superhero Please
Save the Day? . . . . . . . . . . . . . . . . . . . . . . . . . . . . . . . . . . . 161

*Chapter 11:* Release the Beautiful Mom Inside . . . . . . . . . . 175

Resources and Study Guide . . . . . . . . . . . . . . . . . . . . . . . . . 187

Acknowledgments . . . . . . . . . . . . . . . . . . . . . . . . . . . . . . . . . 219

Notes . . . . . . . . . . . . . . . . . . . . . . . . . . . . . . . . . . . . . . . . . . . 221

About the Author . . . . . . . . . . . . . . . . . . . . . . . . . . . . . . . . . 223

# Introduction:

# THE MOM OF MY DAYDREAMS

*I was the perfect mother*—before I had kids.

In my ignorant, childless imagination, motherhood was downright idyllic. I pictured my future cherubs napping at clockwork intervals, swallowing any casserole I set in front of them, and standing motionless while I yanked their curls with a comb.

My brain held happy visions of Chuck E. Cheese outings in which my children would smile wide for Mom's camera and never spill orange soda across the table because, of course, I had no intention of allowing them to drink orange soda. Or root beer. Or lemonade, for goodness' sake. And especially not those neon sugar Pixy Stix peddled from the evil prize counter.

*Only bad moms do that.*

Oh, and my kids wouldn't bonk each other in the forehead with Whac-A-Mole mallets, either.

Not *my* kids.

They'd never bicker. Or roll their eyes. Or beg for marshmallows at breakfast.

My children wouldn't possibly bite other toddlers on the playground or get sent to the principal's office for poking a classmate with a pencil.

And never, ever, *ever* would I plop my precious little people in front of the TV just so I could sneak an uninterrupted shower. Or a nap.

*Only careless, selfish moms do that.* You know—the ones who haven't trained their kids to prefer puzzles over PBS. Sheesh.

Surely I would not be one of those.

In my daydreams, the children of my genes were destined to

be perfect because *I* was determined to be the perfect mom—otherwise known as SuperMom.

But then a life-changing event took place. A single, irreversible episode that would wrestle SuperMom to the ground and choke the ideals right out of her sweet, self-righteous throat. Can you guess what it was?

I gave birth!

To *real* children.

And I soon learned these little people had wills of their own—which often conflicted with *my* will—which then often butt heads with God's will.

And that's when the trouble began.

## THE FIVE-YEAR PLAN

From our wedding day, my husband and I had it all figured out. We'd enjoy five years of child-free honeymoon infatuation, build our careers, stay up late watching Friday-night movies on the couch, then sleep in every Saturday before heading downtown to Starbucks and Home Depot where we'd wander, hand in hand, planning our next house, our next income, our next stage of happily-ever-after.

Parenting began as just a distant goal like so many others. Since planning came naturally to my husband and me, two pragmatic overachievers, we orchestrated high expectations for our family life. Eventually, when we'd had our fill of independence and the five-year finish line came into sight, we cast off our naive contraception and said, "Whoopee, let's go!" And God replied with a resounding *Yes!*—blessing us with a healthy pregnancy from the first cycle we tried.

I spent nine months assuming God deemed me deserving and capable of motherhood.

I was wrong.

Eight hard years later, I now believe God had a different purpose for answering my prayers for children. *He wanted to break me* then build me back up again—stronger, wiser, and far greater blessed than I was before.

## CALLING ALL MOMS LIKE ME

Does your journey through motherhood look different from what you imagined?

Do you struggle to measure up to your own standards?

Do you sometimes wish you could be like that *other* mom who seems to have it all together?

*You are not alone.*

If you've ever looked in the mirror at the end of a hairy day and cursed yourself for yelling, for losing your patience or a permission slip or your ever-elusive sanity.

*I have, too.*

If you give yourself an F for drive-through dinners, carpet stains, or missing your child's soccer goal because your eyes were stuck to your iPhone instead of the field.

*You're more normal than you think.*

If you worry you're warping your kids, or worse, never considered the possibility that you could.

*Then this book is for you.*

Because if you have a child, then you have an assignment from God. Whether by birth or adoption, whether you go to work in an office or the kitchen, regardless of your age or experience or natural talent for nurturing, God has called you to be a mom—and it's an unrelenting, heart-wrenching, beautifully ordinary, *holy* job.

He designed it that way.

And He wants to help you do it—*well*.

This book is for you, my fellow not-so-super moms. The

words you're about to read are born of my own mess-ups, my own heartaches and victories as I fight day after day to seek God in the muck and mundane. These stories will not be foreign to you. Because they're your stories, too—those universal tests and treasures of family life, woven into every momma's backdrop of laundry baskets, minivans, cherry Tylenol, and overdue homework.

So, for the next eleven chapters, won't you please pull up a chair beside me? Let's sip a couple lattes, split a cream cheese brownie, and put our praying heads *together* as we learn from our wise and grace-filled heavenly Father.

He is, after all, the perfect parent. And do you know what that means? The job is already taken. So *we can't have it.* What fantastic news!

# Chapter 1

## WHO ARE THESE LITTLE PEOPLE (AND HOW DO I SEND THEM BACK)?

*Giving birth is little more than a set of muscular contractions granting passage of a child. Then the mother is born.*
ERMA BOMBECK

Remember your first baby shower? Mine was quite an auspicious event. More than fifty women gathered in our church youth hall to usher me into the ranks of motherhood. Fellow newer-married and childless friends cheered me on in solidarity, relishing baby hopes of their own. I'm convinced now that the older women weren't really smiling so much as smirking.

*Oh, that poor dear. She has no freaking clue what's coming.*

Why didn't they speak up?!

I know why. It's the same paralysis of opinion that seizes me now whenever I see a friend's swelling belly and feel compelled to *ooh* and *aah* over the miracle of it all—those tiny fingernails and eyebrows and ear drums, actual working heart valves and kneecaps and kidneys and colons that are *this very moment* being formed inside a beautiful miniature human, which only a God of wonder could sculpt in such intricate detail. Babies are amazing. They're *heavenly art*.

So we tend to focus on the beauty and blessings of a dearly anticipated child, rather than the difficulties to come. After all, blessings make better memories. And pregnancy—first pregnancies in particular—may be one of the most sacred times in a woman's life. Why burst her bubble?

Thus I entered motherhood, wide-eyed as a calf to the veal

factory. At my baby shower, like so many others, I indulged in doting attention from well-meaning ladies. I let them press their palms on my basketball girth. I grinned silly for their cameras. I licked pink frosting and cranberry punch from my bloated prego lips. Then I returned home in a Chevy SUV packed to the ceiling with loot—fleece sleepers, burp rags, bouncy seats, and bum cream.

I stocked duplicates of every supply necessary to care for a child. But I had no idea what it would require of me to raise one.

## CHILDBIRTH IS JUST THE WARM-UP

Have you ever wondered why pregnant women spend so much time and energy preparing for labor? From the moment a pee stick confirms fertile seed, we become consumed with the best way to grow and deliver a baby.

We devour childbirth blogs, magazines, and the latest edition of *What to Expect When You're Expecting*. We research obstetricians, midwives, and doulas within a fifty-mile radius. We drag our husbands to awkward classes on Lamaze and water birth and the Bradley method—and he actually pays attention. As though the process of squeezing a child out of our hoo-haa is the Mount Everest of motherhood.

"Have you been practicing your breathing?" My husband peered over his book one night and pointed this question to me, the swollen heifer on the couch.

"Yes. Sort of." I shrugged.

"You should practice. They said breathing really helps."

"Yes." My mouth spread to a grin. "And so does having a husband who knows how to fetch ice chips and Popsicles." *Like I had any appetite for Popsicles when the hour finally came. Phfft.*

"You put the tennis balls in the suitcase, right?"

"I did. And the gum, and the magazines, and the lip balm."

"And the yoga CD?" *The one prop we actually used.*

"Yes. I think we're good to go."

My husband set his book in his lap and grabbed my fingers. "You're going to do great."

And I did—in childbirth. I was an outright champ. But if you're a mom, then you know labor and delivery are not the mountaintop challenges of parenting. That part is more like a sled hill, or an inclined driveway. Because in return for one or two days of pain and prodding, we earn an eighteen-year birthing process of another kind—our own.

And I don't know of a single class in the world that can prepare women for that.

## DEAR LORD, WHY ARE HER EYES STILL OPEN?

In the hospital, I had no clue how much work the nurses did for me. Every so often they wheeled in a round-face newborn girl, bathed and swaddled, and all I had to do was feed her and stare—at her wispy orange hair poking out from a pink hand-knit cap, at her smooth button nose that so resembled mine. I fell instantly in love with this seven-pound creature, this stranger, the desire of my heart.

So after forty-eight hours as VIP guests in the third-floor birthing suite, my husband and I were eager to get home and *do this* parenting thang. How hard could it be? We'd both changed a diaper in the hospital—check. Our daughter had no trouble latching to my suddenly elastic teats—check. And based on our first two days of experience, our precious babe slept a good four hours at a stretch, so I looked forward to designing cutesy birth announcements between my own indulgent naps. Because, of course, naps were totally on my agenda—check.

On a sleeting early March afternoon, we lifted our daughter's Winnie the Pooh car seat carrier through the front door of our quiet three-bedroom ranch home—her home—and welcomed this child into our real, *forever* life.

And that's when she started wailing.

"What do you think she wants?" I shot a nervous glance at my husband and lifted our daughter from her carrier, watching her tongue vibrate inside a cavernous mouth. *Think, think,* I pep-talked to myself. *The big three—diaper, hunger, gas. Or was it four? Oh, yes, sleepy. Maybe she's sleepy.*

"Let's put her in the bassinet." My husband shifted immediately into male fix-it mode, God bless him. We shushed and snuggled our baby and tucked her in tight to the hand-me-down white lace bassinet that was to be her happy place for the next three months. Or so we thought.

What was I saying about us being overachieving planners? Heh, heh.

*"Many are the plans in a person's heart, but it is the LORD's purpose that prevails" (Proverbs 19:21).*

For the next three or four (*Or was it ten? Twenty?*) weeks, our daughter refused to sleep in her bassinet. Or her crib. Or anyplace that was not Mommy or Daddy's arms. Suddenly this child who was so compliant for the nurses had decided sleep was an unnecessary detail, not only for herself but, consequently, for her desperate parents, too. Each time we attempted ever so carefully to lay her down and tiptoe away, within twenty minutes her eyelids would pop open and she'd start chirping, then crying, then screaming like a mini fire engine. *For weeks on end.* Did I mention that?

We tried *everything*—heartbeat sound effects, swaddling, warming the bassinet mattress with a heating pad. None of it worked. The only way my husband and I managed to catch any rest at all in those first days was by taking turns—one of us flopping on the king-size bed *alone* while the other reclined in a living room chair, sentenced to midnight channel surfing while our baby snuggled in the crook of a cozy, grown-up elbow.

Three days into this shocking routine, we took our daughter to her first doctor's appointment. "Please," I pleaded with the pediatrician, "you have to help us. She doesn't sleep! *We* haven't slept. What's *wrong* with this child? I didn't sign up for this!"

A slow, knowing grin cracked his face. "Every baby is different. Some sleep better than others." He shrugged. "Welcome to parenting!"

*What?* I think I actually felt the sucker punch hit my gut. *That's it?* No remedy, no explanation, no *compassion* for a panicked, crazy woman? He might as well have said, "Well, Mrs. Kopitzke, I'm terribly sorry you've been dealt a vampire child, but hey, suck it up and I'll see you next month for shots!"

That was the first moment I formulated the thought that would plague me often over the coming years.

*What did I get myself into?*

## GOOD-BYE, HUSBAND—ENJOY YOUR NORMAL LIFE AT THE OFFICE

In addition to the inhuman exhaustion, those inaugural months of motherhood presented a series of further twists in our Perfect Parenting Plan. From jaundice to a pitiful milk supply to hormones rushing like white-water rapids, I sank deep into a river of disappointment and tears—mine, not the baby's.

Daily I would stand at the living room window with a pink bundle snuggled in my arms, salt water burning my eyes, and I'd lift a weak hand to wave. My husband waved back from the driveway, escaping to another day at work, another familiar routine involving hot coffee and adult conversation and an hour-long lunch break in which he was not tied to any living thing.

During one of those lunch hours, while on a diaper run to

Target, my husband bumped into a dear friend of mine.

"How is Becky doing?" she asked.

Knowing the level and authenticity of kinship I shared with this woman, my husband let loose the truth. Darn, he probably needed somebody to talk to as much as I did, somebody to help him make sense of his weepy, neurotic wife. "Not so great," he said, and the two of them stood near the checkout sharing a heart-to-heart.

When he came home that evening and told me about his conversation with my friend, my spirits tanked. Not because my husband had revealed the ugly truth about our household, but because *really*? People I love are still out there just wandering the department store, enjoying normal life?

How can this be?

The world was spinning on without me.

And I had never felt so lonely.

## WE ARE NOT ALONE

A year later, God brought me a phone call from this same friend as she sat at home with a three-week-old firstborn of her own.

"How are you doing?" I posed the question gently.

"Fine." The word shook from her mouth.

"No, really. *How are you doing?*"

Instantly her voice broke. She wept. I listened. I encouraged.

"You are not alone." I wanted to reach through the phone and bear hug her. "I know you feel isolated and sad, but that is normal and it *will* pass. I promise you, it will pass."

"Where is the joy?" This plea, the same desperate question I begged from God in my early months, swung toward me like a boomerang. "I thought there was supposed to be so much joy."

My heart ached for my friend, for me, for all the moms who were bamboozled into believing motherhood should be an emotional high. What if it's not? Does that mean there's something wrong with us?

"The joy is hidden," I told her, "but you will find it. I went through the very same thing."

"I know." She sniffled. "I remember. You were honest about what it was like for you, so I felt like I could talk to you about it."

And that's when God first planted this seed in my heart. *Honesty is a ministry.* I grew determined not to let another fellow mother within my influence believe she is alone or failing.

## DON'T LIE TO ME

Not all mothers struggle alike. For me, the newborn season was shockingly hard. Others would gladly trade the toddler or teen years for another shot at those itty bitties.

If your baby hardly cried or snoozed through the night the first week home, or if you have no problem spinning cartwheels on two hours of sleep and every moment of caring for your children is filled with pure joy, then count your blessings and praise the Lord. Sincerely.

If your toddler never bucks your authority or spits out peas, never fights nap time or runs away from you in the Walmart parking lot, great. Consider yourself special.

If your school kids never test your patience, never talk back or beg for candy bars, super. If you enjoy the stomach flu and relish every page of homework stashed in the backpack to complete and sign, terrific!

And if eye-rolling attitudes, teen drama, and all the "Whatever, Mom" comments cast in your general direction do not faze you a bit, then rejoice! You are a rare mother indeed.

Because I am convinced such women are the minority. There are a lot more of us frazzled and frustrated moms of newborns, toddlers, first graders, and freshmen who do *not* have it all together and, sadly, assume *everybody else does* because *women are not talking about it.*

It's time we start being real with one another. Amen?

If you are *ashamed* of your struggles, look up. If you are *unaware* of your struggles or in denial that this book might apply to you, open your eyes. Throughout these pages I'm going to challenge you to consider, *how are you doing in this area?* Tell me anything good, bad, or ugly. But please, please, please—don't lie to me.

We're in this fight together.

Honesty binds us mom to mom, and it invites God to work from the inside out.

*"You deserve honesty from the heart; yes, utter sincerity and truthfulness. Oh, give me this wisdom"* (Psalm 51:6 TLB).

## REDISCOVER THE JOY

So what happened between my husband's Target encounter and the pivotal phone call from my friend one year later? How did I regain perspective, sanity, and zeal for my role as a mom?

*How else?*

God showed up.

He walked with me through the fog until the clouds lifted and I saw Him showering blessings like none I'd experienced before. Motherhood is *hard*, no doubt. God *still* walks with me through the daily crud; He always will. But I'm convinced this parenting journey is also God's greatest tool for chiseling a raw and treasured woman into the masterpiece He sees within.

As my daughter grew, so did I. New challenges popped up every day, and I was constantly forced to a standoff with my own shortcomings. Children are demanding; moms are selfish. Children generate messes; moms hate to clean. Children get sick; I personally fear catching their germs. Children hamper our social lives, our sex lives, our work lives, and our innermost *can-I-just-have-a-minute-to-live-inside-my-own-head-please!* thought lives—if indeed you have any original thoughts left in your brain after a day spent wiping green beans off the floor and singing the VeggieTales theme song over and over and over again.

But, like so many of us, I persevered with God's help. I dug into the Bible for answers to my crankiness, my loneliness, my fatigue, and my fears. I prayed desperately for wisdom and guidance. I pocketed verses that fueled me through long and lonely hours. And as my husband and I celebrated first smiles, first steps, first words, and first birthday candles, we found ourselves living a new rhythm—one in which God's grace sets the tempo. Oh, how we needed Him then, and still do, every undie-changing, lunch-packing, boo-boo kissing day.

Eventually, God blessed us with another baby, the beloved little sister, whom we assimilated into our family adventure with struggles no less soul-stripping than the first. But the second time around, I possessed the gift of insight. God had shown Himself faithful, and I left my doors wide open for His grace.

Today my husband and I are raising two beautiful school-age daughters, and they will be the first to tell you their mother is far from perfect. They've seen my impatience, fallen victim to my worries, withstood my hollering, and witnessed my meltdowns. They've even called me on the carpet a time or two, saying, "Mom, I think we need to ask Jesus to help you." You know it's not an award-winning parenting day when the kids bend a knee on your behalf.

Yet my children have also experienced my bottomless love and tender touch. They've listened to my lullabies and climbed into my lap, where I've wiped countless tears, read bookshelves full of stories, hugged away anxieties, and whispered enough "I love yous" to reach from our overstuffed recliner to heaven's very gate. I'll bet you have, too.

Underneath the chaos and frustrations of family life, we moms cherish our children to the core of our souls. Why is it so hard to show it sometimes? We get cranky, anxious, and overwhelmed. We're too busy, too tired, too ambitious, too distracted. We snap. We nag. We resent and regret, and on bad days we grant our children more pain than peace. How can we prevent those bad days from beating us down?

Think back for a moment to that sense of joy and gratitude you felt at your baby shower. Do you remember when motherhood was a dream come true and not a stressful, sweaty nightmare?

It is possible to reclaim that joy—for ourselves and for the sake of our children.

How?

I've learned through experience, mistakes, prayer, wonderful mentors, and lots of Bible digging. First, identify your villains. Then, with God's strength, rise and conquer!

*"God is our refuge and strength, an ever-present help in trouble"* *(Psalm 46:1).*

## INTRODUCING THE DIRTY VILLAINS OF MOTHERHOOD

Who are these "dirty villains" of motherhood? They're the ugly, sinful tendencies lurking within each mother, poised to take over our good senses and strike against our happy homes. These nasty alter-egos prevent us from enjoying our families and growing closer to God. Their evil powers include

- anger
- worry
- comparison
- busyness

- unhealthy approaches to housework
- exhaustion
- husband-neglect
- self-neglect

If you've faced the dirty villains, you are in good company. All God-fearing women must strengthen their defenses against these beasts—because not a single one of us is immune.

*"If we claim to be without sin, we deceive ourselves and the truth is not in us" (1 John 1:8).*

Through the next eight chapters, we'll examine these dirty villains one by one. We'll discover what compels them to erupt and how we can combat them with biblical wisdom, smart choices, and open communication with God. If you're so inclined, I encourage you to read this book with a small group or trusted friend with whom you can be vulnerable, share your honest struggles, and receive the blessing of support and accountability.

## WHO'S GOT THE POWER?

Imagine for a moment that you are going into battle. It's you versus the dirty villains, and you are determined not to lose this brutal fight. Your family is on the line here, sisters! We're talking serious warfare! So what do you bring? What do you wear? How do you prepare your battle plan?

Examine yourself from the bottom up. First, a woman would probably make sure she has the right shoes. Forget about those fabulous strappy sandals you found on clearance last week; this job calls for steel-toed superhero boots with turbo-charged heels. Low heels, girls. Let's be practical.

Next, you ought to protect your vital organs, so some sort of bulletproof suit would be in order. With moisture-wicking layers, of course. We ladies can be strong *and* unscented.

Now choose a good helmet and some fast-gripping gloves. Pack a canteen of fresh drinking water and a backpack filled with enough freeze-dried spaghetti to last a few days. Throw in a couple chocolate bars just because.

Then grab your weapons—rifles, pistols, swords, stun guns, lightsabers, whatever you imagine your big bad momma self would wield—and fasten them to your belt with extra ammunition.

You're good to go, right?

But wait. One thing is missing.

*The power to fight.*

Where do you get it? What exactly *is* it? If our power isn't in our tools, our intelligence, or even in our fierce will to win, how in the world can a mother grasp what it takes to beat the dirty villains?

The Bible tells us the answer is clear.

Our power comes from God.

> *I pray that the eyes of your heart may be enlightened in order that you may know the hope to which he has called you, the riches of his glorious inheritance in his holy people, and his **incomparably great power for us who believe**. That power is the same as the mighty strength he exerted when he raised Christ from the dead and seated him at his right hand in the heavenly realms. (Ephesians 1:18–20, emphasis added)*

Let's break this passage down a bit so you can see just how important it is.

*"The eyes of your heart may be enlightened."* Fighting the villains is not a matter of brains or brawn. It's a heart issue. Before we can conquer bad habits and sinful tendencies, we must open our hearts to what God wants to teach us.

*"The hope to which he has called you."* Did you know God is calling you? You may not hear an audible voice bellowing down from heaven, but the fact that you've picked up this book shows you're open to receiving a nudge or two from God. That's a great start. He doesn't want you to remain stagnant in your crabby, selfish, or worrying ways. God has a better offer, and He's inviting you to take it.

*"The riches of his glorious inheritance."* This messy world is not the end of the road. A glorious inheritance awaits us, and not just in heaven! God wants to give us hope for *this* life as well as the life to come.

*"Incomparably great power."* Um, God created the entire world in six days. I'd say *powerful* is an understatement. Imagine if you could tap God's unparalleled strength in your battle against the dirty villains.

Great news! You can!

*"For us who believe."* This is the key. For us who believe. Believe what? Believe in our smarts? Our determination? Our weapons? Our fancy turbo boots?

Nope.

In order for any of the principles we're about to explore in this book to work; in order for any of your efforts to bear fruit; in order for the words you read in these chapters to stick, I mean really *stick*—you must first believe on Jesus.

*"For every child of God defeats this evil world, and we achieve this victory through our faith. And who can win this battle against the world? Only those who believe that Jesus is the Son of God"* *(1 John 5:4–5 NLT).*

Without Jesus, our battle gear is useless. We might as well show up at the villainous fight buck naked. But *with* Jesus, we're not only equipped to face the challenges of this world—we're also granted the wonderful assurance of eternal life in heaven. This is called the gift of salvation, and it's absolutely free.

*"For the wages of sin is death, but the gift of God is eternal life in Christ Jesus our Lord" (Romans 6:23).*

Here's the deal. We're all born with villains. They're called our sin nature, passed down from Adam and Eve. I like to blame Eve sometimes for eating that darn apple, but the truth is, if I'd been in her footsteps, I might've done the very same thing. Admit it, you might've, too.

Those villains separate us from God. He is perfect, so He cannot be near anything blemished or sinful. That would be a serious bummer if it weren't for one vital factor. God provided a solution: Jesus.

We just read in Romans 6 that "the wages of sin is death," which means sin requires punishment, and somebody has to take it. That's where Jesus comes in. God sent Jesus into this world to live the perfect life we cannot live, and to die the death that should have been ours. If we choose to follow Jesus—to surrender control of our own lives to Him (which sounds like a good bargain if you really consider how *not* well you've been doing at running your own life, eh?)—then *Bam!*—God sends Jesus, in the form of the Holy Spirit, to live inside of us. And now when God looks at us, He doesn't see the sin. He only sees Jesus—perfect, beautiful, holy Jesus. And we're reconciled to God forever.

*"For God so loved the world that he gave his one and only Son, that whoever believes in him shall not perish but have eternal life" (John 3:16).*

Why am I telling you all this? Because it's critical to our process. Without the power of Jesus living inside you, nothing in this book will truly come to life in your heart and in your household. Some of you may already know Jesus as your Lord and Savior. If you're not sure, then chances are, you don't. And I would be blessed to share an opportunity with you today to hand your life, your struggles, your joy and your pain over to Jesus—where you will be in the ultimate safest keeping. Then together we can slay those dirty villains for good.

Will you pray with me?

*Heavenly Father, I confess I've made mistakes. I've tried to run my own life; I've neglected to call on You or to give You the rightful place You deserve in my heart. Father, please forgive me. Today I surrender myself to You—my hopes, my dreams, my fears, and my failures. Lord, will You please take them and turn them into something beautiful and trustworthy? I believe You sent Your Son, Jesus, to die for me. I want to accept Your free gift of salvation. I am Yours. Please give me Your Holy Spirit to guide me and secure me among Your beloved children. I pray this in the name of Jesus. Amen.*

# Chapter 2

## THE GROUCH ON THE COUCH

*Sometimes you don't realize you
have a temper until you have kids.*
LISA-JO BAKER

**Dirty Villain No. 1:** The Grouch on the Couch
**Evil Powers:** Anger, impatience, yelling, irritability,
lack of self-control
**Kryptonite:** Proverbs 29:11; James 1:19–20; Proverbs 28:13;
Ephesians 6:10–17; Ephesians 4:26–27; Proverbs 22:15;
Psalm 86:15; Psalm 119:11; Proverbs 14:1; Proverbs 15:1;
Proverbs 15:3; 1 Corinthians 13:4; John 3:17

---

*D*ad, why is Mom so cranky?" My seven-year-old daughter
posed this question to my husband one evening while they
sat feet-up on the living room couch watching the Food Network.

"I don't know, sweetheart, why do you ask?"

"Because she yelled at me when we were making popcorn,
and I don't know why."

"Oh, Mom didn't mean it." My husband shook his head.
"She's just tired."

"Yeah, Dad. I think she needs more sleep. Because Mom is
*always* cranky."

Ouch.

When my husband relayed this conversation to me the next
day, it stabbed my heart—but my daughter was right. Somehow in the daily grind of child care, housework, deadlines, and

more housework, I had morphed into a cranky version of myself, spring-loaded to bark at anybody who crossed my path.

Oh, I collect plenty of excuses for my grouchy mom moments. The house is too noisy for my introverted psyche. I'm weary from a long and busy day. My to-do list is out of control. I've got a lot on my mind, okay, people? And if these kids would just cooperate and brush their teeth and pick up their crayons and stop climbing on the sofa *when they're told*, for crying out loud—then I wouldn't have to be so crabby!

Right?

Well. . .not exactly.

Proverbs 29:11 tells us, *"Fools give full vent to their rage, but the wise bring calm in the end."*

Understand this verse does *not* say, "A fool feels rage." Anger and irritation are not necessarily sins in themselves; even Jesus got angry sometimes. Psalm 7:11 (NLT) confirms, "God is an honest judge. He is angry with the wicked every day."

Whoa! What a relief to know God gets ticked off, too! But— *"My dear brothers and sisters, take note of this: Everyone should be quick to listen, slow to speak and slow to become angry, because human anger does not produce the righteousness that God desires"* (James 1:19–20).

Do you see the difference? God has righteous anger. We have human anger, which means it's inherently faulty. Even when the cause of our anger is justified, *how we deal with it* can quickly become a problem. What does it look like to "give full vent" to our anger?

- yelling
- snapping
- criticizing people we love
- physical outbursts, such as throwing objects or impulsive spanking

Lovely stuff, eh?

Of all the dirty villains of motherhood, the Grouch on the Couch is my most frequent visitor. I used to make excuses for her behavior as though she were only passing through. Until one day, a friend set me straight.

"I'm just in a rough season," I told her. My schedule at that particular time had tripped well beyond the threshold of a twenty-four-hour day, overstuffed with writing deadlines and church ministry, plus it was the end of the school year—and the list of parties and paperwork and field trips to keep track of was seriously chafing my nerves. "It's like one thing on top of another is crowding my white space and making me a little cuckoo, right?" My eyes widened and I looked to my friend for empathy. "But it's just a season. I'll pull through!"

Her reply?

"Becky, you've been in that season for a long time."

*Aha*. Stunned, the lights inside my head flickered on. Suddenly I saw my own life in true color for the first time in months, maybe years.

Grouchy had become my norm.

How about you? Is the Grouch on the Couch an occasional invader or a live-in guest? Bad days are understandable. We all have them, and God's grace blows through the house to help pick up our mess and start fresh the next morning. But when one bad day transitions to another and another and another *ad infinitum*, that's no longer just a bad day.

That's a legacy.

If your children have come to define you as a perpetual crank, it's not too late to reinvent yourself. I've discovered— the hard way—six tricks to conquering the Grouch. And yes, they actually work. Take it from a woman who used to speak Hollering as her native language. Thanks to these tricks, drawn straight from the Bible, I've recovered my fluency in tranquil English. Let's examine these strategies, embrace them, and implement them. Then together we'll give that Grouch on the Couch a good, swift kick out the door.

## 1. Acknowledge the Grouch

Have you seen *The Incredible Hulk*? There's always that scene where some cardiac trigger converts mild-mannered Bruce Banner, the Hulk's alter ego, into a ghastly beast, and involuntarily his eyes burn an evil green while the bulging force of his fury rips his shirt at the seams.

I wish we moms had such an obvious transformation. It would be much easier to recognize the Grouch when she arrives and to give her the acknowledgment she's due. *Oops! My biceps just turned a strange mossy color and I'm sprouting hair from my nostrils—must be time to count to ten!*

Typically, however, that nasty villain creeps up on us, almost imperceptibly, after a long week of diaper changing, hormone wrangling, school-to-soccer carpooling, or rushing home from work to feed hungry people with nothing but two apples and three hot dogs in the fridge. And the Grouch pounces without warning or permission. This happens to me often, but the first time I truly detected it was one Saturday morning a few years ago, when my husband pulled into our garage with a trunk full of groceries.

Of course, I was grateful. Back in those days, my sweet man willingly took over the shopping so I didn't have to juggle two little supermarket companions during the week. I'd write the list, and he'd wheel through the aisles at sunrise collecting the goods. What a deal.

So when he hauled bags into the kitchen and I began unloading, I batted my lashes in dreamy gratitude. *Awww, he bought my favorite bagels. My hero.*

My husband settled in a kitchen chair to sip coffee and scan the newspaper while I stacked tuna cans and hummed a cheery tune. Our girls sat beside their dad slurping chocolate milk and Cheerios. We were a billboard of domestic peace.

Until I opened my trap.

"Honey, where are the diapers?"

He jerked his head from the paper, eyes wide, and blinked. "What diapers? They weren't on the list."

Slowly, I ran a fingertip down the crumpled shopping list to ensure I wasn't about to perjure myself. Right there in my tidy penmanship, under the bold "Baby Aisle" header, glowed the word *Diapers*.

"Yes, they were."

"Oh, I'm sorry, honey. I missed it."

All at once, blood bubbled from my toes to my forehead. "You *missed* it? We buy diapers every week."

"Well, then, you should do the shopping next time. You're better at it."

I squeezed my eyelids shut, dug my fingernails into my palms, and squelched the urge to scream. *Aaaaaaaaaaaaaaaaaack! He forgot the diapers? Where has he been for the last five years! We are diaper people! My husband is useless! I hate my life!*

Hold on a second. That's not true. How could such terrible thoughts pop into my brain?

Ah—of course. The Grouch had arrived. And she aimed to take over.

*Welcome, you nasty old hag.*

The first step to conquering the Grouch is *acknowledging her presence in the room.* Recognize that your frustration is an object you can identify and control; it does not have to control you.

Likewise, ignoring the Grouch, stuffing her down, or pretending she doesn't exist can ultimately harm us and everybody around us. We become like pressure cookers, building steam until our tops blow and splatter boiling droplets of frustration all over the people we love best.

The Grouch *will* bust out one way or another. We're better off acknowledging her presence before she swallows our self-control. Then once that dirty villain is exposed, we can see her more clearly in our crosshairs.

*"Whoever conceals their sins does not prosper, but the one who confesses and renounces them finds mercy" (Proverbs 28:13).*

## 2. Know Who Your Real Enemy Is—It's Not Your Kids

*Finally, be strong in the Lord and in his mighty power.*
*Put on the full armor of God, so that you can take your*
*stand against the devil's schemes. For our struggle is not*
*against flesh and blood, but against the rulers, against the*
*authorities, against the powers of this dark world and*
*against the spiritual forces of evil in the heavenly realms.*
*(Ephesians 6:10–12)*

I don't give a lot of credit to Satan. He's a defeated foe since God has already "disarmed the powers and authorities" and "made a public spectacle of them, triumphing over them by the cross" (Colossians 2:15). But let's not be deceived. "God is love" (1 John 4:8), therefore Satan is thrilled when we act unlovingly.

*"'In your anger do not sin': Do not let the sun go down while you are still angry, and do not give the devil a foothold" (Ephesians 4:26–27).*

When our kids irritate us, do they become our enemies? When our husbands grind us down, are they suddenly the adversary? Of course not. We're family. We're on the same team.

However, when we let anger and frustration chip away at the

glue that binds us, the Bible says we're giving Satan a foothold. "Do not let the sun go down while you are still angry" in essence means, don't invite the Grouch to take up permanent residence in your home and in your heart. We must not allow grudges to form or fester within our own families, because they create cracks where Satan can seep in.

One of the most effective tricks I've found for fighting the Grouch is this simple sentence—a mantra—that unfailingly whips my perspective back into shape.

*I will not let Satan get my family.*

When my children climb the furniture and break a photo frame.

*I will not let Satan get my family.*

When my daughter melts in a pool of adolescent drama and requires my emotional presence, not my impatience.

*I will not let Satan get my family.*

When my husband hurts me with thoughtless words or his own distracted priorities.

*I will not let Satan get my family.*

Try reciting that conviction in the heat of an argument and see if it doesn't soften your heart. Nothing is worth sacrificing the people we love best to an enemy who knows nothing of love. *Nothing.*

## 3. Discern Age-Appropriate Behavior

Now that we know who we're dealing with, it's important to keep the right perspective. What's triggering your grouchiness? Are the kids bickering? Making too much noise? Refusing to cooperate with your seventeenth command to *put their shoes on, already*? Before we react, we must ask ourselves one vital question:

Is this age-appropriate behavior?

When my seven-year-old twirls her baton in the living room

and accidentally whacks me across the forehead, do I get angry? Yes. But is that normal behavior for a seven-year-old? It is.

When my four-year-old begs to eat Popsicles three meals a day, does that irritate Mommy? It sure does. But is it common testing from a child her age? Indeed.

If your preteen stays up too late reading and won't wake up for church or your sophomore loses the car keys, do you get mad? Maybe so. But then perhaps you also committed those same offenses just last week. How can you show no mercy?

Proverbs 22:15 tells us, *"Folly is bound up in the heart of a child, but the rod of discipline will drive it far away."*

What does that verse say to you? I catch two distinct points:

(1) "Folly is bound up in the heart of a child." Amen! Chances are our kids aren't being naughty just to spite us. Foolishness is part of their condition. It's normal. And yet it's not supposed to be permanent because (2) "the rod of discipline will drive it far away."

That's our part. As parents, we are called to correct the folly—to teach our children the way they should go, so when they are old they will not turn from it (Proverbs 22:6). Most moms I know pour their aching souls into the task. We train. We correct. We reinforce. We encourage. So when our hard work crumbles into tantrums and disobedience, it's easy to point fingers at our children or, worse, at our own performance as parents.

But there's a flaw in that thinking.

Our kids aren't puppets; they're people. They're born with the same sin nature as ours and the same free will to make their own decisions. We all know how well that works for us sometimes. Can we really expect more from our kids than we do from ourselves?

We can't control their hearts. We can only control our response.

When they act like kids—foolish, naughty, selfish—let's remind ourselves that, yes, that is indeed what they are. Kids. On a long journey to maturity. They're learning just like we are.

"I think I finally know how God feels," a friend told me one day when we were comparing battle wounds from unruly children. "I disobey Him all the time. And he has a lot more patience with me than I do with my kids."

*"But you, Lord, are a compassionate and gracious God, slow to anger, abounding in love and faithfulness" (Psalm 86:15).*

Let's follow God's lead, amen? He knows our limitations and our faults, yet He is kind to us. Can we do the same for our kids? Next time the children act up, ask yourself, "Is this age-appropriate behavior?" If so, it might require compassionate training rather than grouchy punishment. God's grace is huge. Let's lavish the overflow onto our kids.

## 4. The Quick-Switch Trick

I confess to having a little *volume* problem. Do you? I've come a long way, but there was a time when yelling and snapping was my default response to stressful situations. As moms, when circumstances collide with our tired, preoccupied, or controlling state of mind, any shred of virtuous restraint remaining within us can easily blow up and spew out our mouths. I call this "verbal vomit." It's a debilitating disease. I suffered from it for several years.

In *Psychology Today*, Ohio State University psychology professor Brad Bushman explained:

> *Venting anger is like using gasoline to put out a fire: It just feeds the flame. Venting keeps arousal levels high and keeps aggressive thoughts and angry feelings alive. Maybe you have heard of the joke, "How do you get to Carnegie Hall?" The answer is: "Practice! Practice! Practice!" My question to you is: "How do you become an angry, aggressive person?"*

*The answer is the same: "Practice! Practice! Practice!" Venting is just practicing how to behave more aggressively, such as by hitting, kicking, screaming, and shouting.*[1]

So what's the solution? We've already established it's not a good idea to stuff our anger. But it doesn't help to spew it, either. Psychologists suggest the best approach is to get rid of the anger altogether. This prevents harm to ourselves and the people around us. But how?

Introducing the Quick Switch.

The concept is simple. Whenever you're tempted to snap, immediately replace the angry thought with scripture. Does it work? Yes. But don't take my word for it. Take God's.

*"I have hidden your word in my heart that I might not sin against you" (Psalm 119:11).*

"Honey," I told my husband one Sunday afternoon, "I'm going downstairs to pay bills. Can you keep an eye on the girls for a while?"

"Uh-huh." My husband reclined in a playroom chair and rustled the newspaper. Our daughters scurried around him, leaping off their indoor trampoline and pounding drumsticks onto Rubbermaid lids. I paused for a second to admire my newly vacuumed rug then grabbed my checkbook and headed for the basement office.

Half an hour later, I ventured back upstairs. I waltzed across the kitchen, turned a corner toward the playroom, and froze.

Disaster. Everywhere.

Toy bins sat upturned and empty. Stuffed animals, tea set utensils, and Happy Meal gadgets lay strewn over the carpet and tossed onto furniture. Sofa cushions were stripped from their seats and stacked double high on the floor beneath heaps of coloring books, crumpled construction paper, half-eaten apples, and markers without caps.

"What is all this?" I stared at the mess, appalled.

"We built a toy store, Momma," one of my daughters called from down the hall. Dad and his skippers had already fled the shipwreck and lounged in the master bedroom watching television. I lifted my eyes from the floor to the wall. Post-it notes were stuck four feet up, scrawled with the letters, TOY MARKET OPEN.

Rising from deep in my belly, I sensed the urge to roar. *Bwwwwwaaaaaahhhh!* Half an hour! *I step away for* half *an hour and this is what I get?! Do you think I have nothing better to do than clean up this mess? Pay the bills* yourself *next time, husband! I'll stay up here and take scissors to your hunting magazines! Aaaaaaaaaack!*

Verbal vomit is nasty junk. Once that stuff splats out, it clings to hurt feelings and leaves tough stains all over the house. If only we women could get our hands on a preventive drug for freaking out.

We can. It's called scripture.

Twice, with fists clenched, I stomped toward the television to unleash fury on my husband. The Grouch was on *fire* to shout it all out.

But I didn't.

Because each time I opened my mouth to yell, these priceless words burst in my head and dripped down my throat, squelching the urge to purge:

*"Fools give full vent to their rage" (Proverbs 29:11).*

*"The wise woman builds her house, but with her own hands the foolish one tears hers down" (Proverbs 14:1).*

So I turned around, clamped my lips, and let the steam blow out my nose.

That day, I claimed a small victory. Instead of spewing hurtful words at my husband—in front of the kids, for shame, for shame—I obeyed God's Word. And the results were amazing.

Anger escaped my body with each breath. The Grouch, that mad beast, evaporated. Suddenly, armed with scripture, I laughed at my own absurdity. My kids had a blast playing with their dad. He lets our girls have the fun I prevent in the name of tidiness. He's good for them. And? That playroom mess was nothing compared to the wreckage I nearly created with my tongue.

I didn't stuff. I didn't vent. I effectively eliminated my anger from the situation—for real. All thanks to the Quick Switch.

God's Word is our greatest weapon in the battle against the Grouch. God tells us this Himself in the book of Ephesians. Let's look at the rest of the "full armor of God" passage we examined earlier in this chapter.

> *Therefore put on the full armor of God, so that when the day of evil comes, you may be able to stand your ground, and after you have done everything, to stand. Stand firm then, with the belt of truth buckled around your waist, with the breastplate of righteousness in place, and with your feet fitted with the readiness that comes from the gospel of peace. In addition to all this, take up the shield of faith, with which you can extinguish all the flaming arrows of the evil one. Take the helmet of salvation and **the sword of the Spirit, which is the word of God.** (Ephesians 6:13–17, emphasis added)*

Notice every piece of armor—belt, breastplate, shoes, shield, helmet—is a defensive weapon, with one exception: the Word of God. That's a sword—the only *offensive* weapon in the bunch. This should tell us how powerful God's Word truly is and how we're meant to wield it. Do you want to slay the Grouch on the Couch? Then fill your arsenal with scripture—and use it every chance you get.

## 5. Put a Little Love in Your Voice

My mom has a saying—*put a little love in your voice*. It's her advice to my sisters and me when she hears us crabbing at our kids.

If only she could be in my house at seven thirty every morning to remind me.

"Are you done with your breakfast?" I call down the hall to my daughters on a typical weekday. "It's time to brush your teeth! Hurry or we'll be late for school."

Imagine those words poured sweet as syrup from a momma's lips. The inner dialogue sings, *"Sweetie pie, did you get your fill of pancakes? My heart aches to think of you hungry at recess. Off you go now to brush-a-brush those pearly whites! Let's make sure you have plenty of time to hang your backpack and change out of your snow boots before the bell rings. Love you!"*

If it were anybody else talking to my child, that's the tone of voice I'd want to hear.

Why, then, do I often sound like this?

*"Are you* still *poking at your breakfast? Look at the clock, for crying out loud! Hightail it to the sink and brush your teeth* now*! Don't make me drive like a wailing ambulance to get your lazy bottom to school on time! Move!"*

Yikes. Do you see? The trouble isn't necessarily *what* the Grouch says. It's *how* she says it.

*"A gentle answer turns away wrath, but a harsh word stirs up anger"* (Proverbs 15:1).

Oh, how many emotional disasters could be averted in our homes if we'd just put a little love in that voice. Haven't we moms figured out by now that impatience is counterproductive? When I bark at my kids, they tune me out at best. Sometimes they strike back. Worst, on rare but awful occasions, they cry. Then I grovel in the driver's seat all the way to school, wishing for a do-over.

So I took my mom's advice one day. Whenever frustration bubbled within me and threatened to spurt, I blew the air from my lungs and spoke gently instead.

"No, you cannot have a lollipop for breakfast."

Not: *"Are you serious? You just woke up two minutes ago and already you're begging for sugar? What is wrong with you?"*

But rather: *"Oh, you're so silly! I've got something better. Strawberries, yay!"*

"I told you to put your jacket on."

Not: *"For the last time, get your stupid jacket on!"*

But rather: *"Um, remember? I mentioned that little jacket thing a minute ago. Let's try again."*

"Buckle your seat belt!"

Not: *"Quit squirming in your seat and focus, people! We need to go!"*

But rather: *"Alrighty, happy campers, let's all buckle up for safety!"*

And guess what—it worked. My girls cooperated more readily, found fewer opportunities to buck me, and everyone hopped into the minivan, smiling and chatty, three minutes ahead of schedule.

Amazing.

I find it interesting that a few lines down in the book of Proverbs, after the verse about gentle answers versus harsh words, shines this little gem:

*"The eyes of the LORD are everywhere, keeping watch on the wicked and the good" (Proverbs 15:3).*

Do you ever wonder if you'd act differently with Jesus in the room? Hey, I'd spiff up my behavior if the *mailman* stopped by. Imagine how far I'd go to tame my tongue for the Lord of the universe.

And that's the kicker. God *is* in the room. His eyes are in our kitchens when we're mopping spilled juice. He's in our hallways when we're wrestling octopus arms into jackets. He travels in our vehicles when the kids bicker over what carpool game to play. *I spy? Or rhyming words? I know, kids—let's ask Jesus!*

Thankfully, the Lord is full of grace. He loves us through our harsh words and do-over mornings. But I wonder—if we wouldn't snap at Jesus to hurry and brush His teeth, why should our kids deserve less?

*Put a little love in your voice.* It's Proverbs 15:1, paraphrased mom-style. Start with the morning routine, then, if you dare, expand the practice to your bedtime rituals. The Grouch will have no key times of day left in which to strike. Imagine how that could drastically change your household for the better.

## 6. Learn to Apologize

I often write these words on my kitchen chalkboard as a reminder:

*"Love is patient, love is kind" (1 Corinthians 13:4).*

Take a look around. I'm betting that in your house right now live the people you love best. Therefore, they should be granted the greatest claims on your kindness. Not your grouchiness.

The Grouch on the Couch is not patient. She is not kind. So far we've explored five effective tricks to conquering this dirty villain, and together they can severely incapacitate her ability to inflict harm.

However, no mom is perfect, and we're all bound to slip, maybe even tomorrow—or today. The key is to be aware of how our words, actions, and attitudes are stacking up—even in the midst of constant external pressures—and to make deliberate efforts to pile on more patience than pestering, more smiles than spewing, more softness than snits, and more hugs than hollers.

Then even when we mess up, we still have one tool left in our Grouch-fighting kit.

The power of an apology.

Author Kristen Strong, on her blog *Chasing Blue Skies*, wrote, "Proverbs 3:34 says the Lord gives grace to the humble. When we apologize to our kids, we show humility and invite grace into our homes, and heaven knows everyone wants to reside in a house where grace lives."[2]

Isn't that the truth? Throughout scripture, God exhorts us to forgive one another—for good reasons. Yes, because He forgave us first (Ephesians 4:32) and because unforgiveness hinders our relationship with God (Matthew 6:14–15). But as moms, we need to take the necessity of forgiveness one step further and realize what it says to our children. When we apologize and ask our kids for forgiveness, it teaches them that we are not perfect, nor do we expect them to be. Genuine apologies create an atmosphere of mutual grace, where kids and parents alike can feel free to make mistakes without condemnation. And that, my fellow moms, paints the very picture of Jesus for our children.

*"For God did not send his Son into the world to condemn the world, but to save the world through him" (John 3:17).*

# Chapter 3

# WORRY MUCH?

*Parts of us crack wide open, and we are vulnerable to a vast army of fears, for to parent is to ache over the unknown.*
Lisa-Jo Baker

**Dirty Villain No. 2:** Worry Woman
**Evil Powers:** Fear, worry, overprotecting, controlling
**Kryptonite:** 2 Timothy 1:7; Jeremiah 17:9; Proverbs 4:23;
  Proverbs 28:26; James 1:5; Psalm 139:1–6; Proverbs 3:13–18;
  Proverbs 1:8–9; Romans 8:38–39; Romans 8:28;
  Proverbs 3:5–6; Matthew 26:39; Psalm 37:5

———

She mounted the twisted iron ladder to the monkey bars. Surely she could slip and smack her nose. So I yelled to my daughter before she reached the second rung. "Be careful!"

Later she danced in the living room, twirling to her heart's content. "Be careful," I warned. "You'll get dizzy." In my mind, every piece of furniture stood waiting to collide with her head.

At dinnertime, she asked to pour the milk herself. I promise I won't spill, she said. "All right," I acquiesced, and yet the caution flag flew out of my mouth for the hundredth time that day. "Please—be careful." *Accidents are not on my agenda today!*

Do you say it, too? Two common, careless words, a staple battle cry in the loving mother's lexicon.

*Be careful!*

*Be careful!*

Please, *would you just be careful?*

What are we so afraid of?

Whether you've been parenting for a decade or a day, you know firsthand how momma-bear instincts run deep and wide. We moms sniff out danger at every turn, fiercely protecting our cubs from threats both real and imagined. Hey, it's our job, right? God entrusted these children to our care, so by golly, we are determined not to mess it up.

Therefore we teach our kids to be cautious. But do they also know how to be brave?

*"For the Spirit God gave us does not make us timid, but gives us power, love and self-discipline" (2 Timothy 1:7).*

In recent years, I've come to realize the phrase "be careful" can do more harm than good. Yes, we want to instill a sense of awareness in our children, and it is our duty as parents to nurture and protect—to a certain degree. But isn't it also our job to empower our children? To provide for them a launchpad from which they'll jump into the skins God designed for them?

Our next enemy, Worry Woman, can choke the life from both parent and child faster than any other dirty villain we face. Worry inhibits our ability to enjoy our children, and it instills in our kids a sense of fear that hinders them from exploring beyond their parents' emotional confines. Do you enjoy worrying? I sure hope not. Does it make you feel strong? More likely it weakens your spirit. So why would we purposely impart this same debility to our children?

We wouldn't. And that's the problem. Often we're not aware of Worry Woman's effect on our kids until the damage has already been done.

If your goal is to raise a timid child, I can offer a few tips—from experience.

- Say, "Be careful," more than you say, "I believe in you."

- Pray for your child's safety more than you pray for her character.
- Fear the world more than you trust God.

Terrible, isn't it? I'm fanatical about keeping my children safe. I want to spare them pain. Yet, beneath my anxious surface, what I really want most for them is *faith*—to love and follow Christ with unswerving devotion. That kind of life is meaningful beyond measure, but it may not necessarily be *safe*.

Sometimes God asks us to take risks. Bold faith requires stretching beyond what's comfortable or certain. What if God's plan for our children involves traveling to faraway places? What if it requires chasing an impossible dream or discovering a cure for cancer or jumping out of airplanes?

*What if they are to become parents themselves?* Such a calling is not for the faint of heart. Our kids are going to need some serious moxie. And how will they get it if we never let them taste adventure?

The process of instilling courage in our kids begins with breaking free from our own worry woes. From now on, let's change that battle cry from "Be careful" to "Be brave!"

## EQUIPPING OUR CHILDREN FROM THE INSIDE OUT
What is the greatest threat to your child's well-being? Counter to what many parents fear, it's not their surroundings or external influences. The Bible tells us a child's greater danger comes from within his or her own heart. *"The heart is deceitful above all things and beyond cure. Who can understand it?"* (Jeremiah 17:9).

The best action we can take to protect our children is to teach them about God. He alone can change hearts—and save our children from themselves—when they embrace Jesus as their Savior (2 Corinthians 5:17). So make it a priority to pray with your children. Explore Bible stories and memorize verses together. Point to God in everything you do and see. And teach your kids to protect their hearts from anything that would draw them away from God. *"Above all else, guard your heart, for everything you do flows from it"* (Proverbs 4:23).

## THE ART AND SCIENCE OF LETTING GO

Fear and worry are compound problems, because they often lead to another issue—control-freak tendencies. Worry Woman believes if she can just control the circumstances surrounding her children, she can prevent poor choices, which will consequently prevent harm and heartache for everyone.

Does it really work that way?

No. In fact, this strategy often backfires. But you have to hand it to her, Worry Woman tries—desperately. Let's explore three common areas in which many of us struggle to let go.

### 1. Growing Up—The natural progression to school and independence

For the first two weeks of kindergarten, my older daughter cried every day at lunch because she missed me. My aching mommy heart longed to yank her out of school and indulge her with chocolate ice-cream cones in the safety of our fenced backyard.

But I didn't.

Why?

Because the less she leans on me, the more she'll need to lean on God. And that is the ultimate goal of parenting.

*"Those who trust in themselves are fools, but those who walk in wisdom are kept safe"* (Proverbs 28:26).

Conventional parenting wisdom says we ought to raise our kids to be independent, to rely on their smarts and strength. But that's not a biblical view. Quite the opposite, I want my children to be increasingly *dependent*—on God, the source of true wisdom. Don't you want that for your kids, too? Unfortunately for Worry Woman, learning to lean on God means giving our children room to grow and stumble. By doing so, we set the example that Mom depends on God first—to take care of them.

It's not easy.

*"If any of you lacks wisdom, you should ask God, who gives generously to all without finding fault, and it will be given to you" (James 1:5).*

For the remainder of that kindergarten year, I set an alarm at 11:45 every weekday to pray for my daughter's courage. As she marched to the lunchroom in a school across town, separated from me by city streets yet connected heart to heart through the same God who watched over us both, I lifted her up to her gentle Shepherd. Some days my prayers sounded more like whine fests.

*Lord, what if she's sad? What if she needs me? Will anyone see? Will anyone care? Nobody at that school loves her like I do!*

Oh, really? Says who?

*LORD, you have seen what is in my heart. You know all about me. You know when I sit down and when I get up. You know what I'm thinking even though you are far away. You know when I go out to work and when I come back home. You know exactly how I live. LORD, even before I speak a word, you know all about it. You are all around me, behind me and in front of me. You hold me safe in your hand. I'm amazed at how well you know me. It's more than I can understand. (Psalm 139:1–6 NIrV)*

Before we can let go of our children, we must remember to *whom* they're going. We're not really handing them over to school, or to softball practice, summer camp, or sleepovers. We're giving them first to God. He sees them when we can't. He reads their minds when we only wish we had a clue. Even their hurt is somehow under His purposeful control.

Because He *holds them in His hand.*

Wow. Do we really think we can do better?

It's a radical truth: no matter how much we love our kids, God loves them more. I can hardly comprehend it. And—God loves *us* that much, too.

He sees every pathetic Worry Woman pouting in the kitchen, fretting over her child's first job, first date, first recital, first steps. And He invites us to toss those heavy burdens into the arms of our Savior who says, *Nobody loves your child like I do. Trust Me.*

My daughter eventually overcame her homesickness, thanks to a breakthrough one day on the drive to school. She was singing her favorite Sunday school song with gusto. "Be strong! Joshua 1:9! Be strong and courageous, do not be terrified. Do not be discouraged, for the LORD your God is with you wherever you go!"

"Sweetheart, that's it!" I shouted from the driver's seat. "You can sing that song to yourself when you're walking to lunch. For the Lord your God is with you—even in the cafeteria!"

"Yeah!" Her eyes sparkled wide and she smiled. "I'll try it!" That afternoon when she boarded our minivan at pick-up time, my soul rejoiced to hear these beautiful words: "It worked, Mom! I didn't cry! God helped me be brave!"

By the end of the year, my daughter hardly tossed me a "Bye, Mom" before disappearing through the school doors for the best hours of her day. And I was grateful.

Not because she didn't need me. But because she was learning where her real strength lies.

Who do you want your children to depend on, ultimately?

You or God? Worry Woman would like to believe she's doing God's bidding by rolling her children in bubble wrap and squashing their heads so they can neither grow nor escape into the big, bad world. But that's not quite what God ordered. He has a plan for our children just as He does for each of us moms. And His plan involves growing *up* and *out* and *into* God's will for their lives. There is no safer destination for our children. What a privilege we have to usher them there.

## 2. Decision Making—Empowering our kids to make wise choices

As my daughters grow, I'm learning to let them make their own choices. Even when Worry Woman disagrees. Like one memorable Saturday, for example, at the grocery store.

"Mom, can we get a watermelon? Please? Please? I love watermelon!" My then six-year-old spied a crate of enormous melons in the center of the produce aisle. She clasped her hands in front of her chest, pleading.

"Sure, we can get a watermelon." I nodded. "If you promise me you're going to eat it."

"I will, I will! Can I pick one?"

"Umm... Ooookay."

Now, you need to understand—I'm really picky about my fruit. Grapes must be firm, apples need green stems, bananas should be slender, and watermelons are best in smooth, sun-ripened skins.

So when my daughter reached for the ugliest, pock-marked, asymmetrical, yellow watermelon in the pile, I cringed.

"You like that one?" I raised my eyebrows.

"Yeah, Momma, I want this watermelon."

I hovered over the crate for a few seconds, dropped my jaw halfway to object, then clamped it and exhaled hard through my nose. I helped my daughter lift her choice into the cart and wheeled toward the bakery aisle without looking back.

It's only a watermelon, after all. Not a car or a college or a husband. Can't hurt to let her pick her own fruit, right? Might even help.

> *Blessed are those who find wisdom, those who gain understanding, for she is more profitable than silver and yields better returns than gold. She is more precious than rubies; nothing you desire can compare with her. Long life is in her right hand; in her left hand are riches and honor. Her ways are pleasant ways, and all her paths are peace. She is a tree of life to those who take hold of her; those who hold her fast will be blessed. (Proverbs 3:13–18)*

Our kids will make a lot of choices in their lifetimes. What clothes to wear, which friends to hang out with, whether to say yes or no to drugs. I have opinions about these things, of course, and in some cases my opinions dictate rules for my children to follow. But eventually their decisions won't be under my sole influence or happening under my roof. When that time comes, I hope and pray to God they'll do the right thing.

But how? How will our children learn to make wise choices if we constantly make their decisions for them? Yes, a watermelon is only a watermelon. But at that moment, it was so much more. It was an opportunity—to show my daughter that her decisions matter.

One day, each of our children will make the ultimate choice—whether or not to live for Jesus. Let's start now, building our kids' confidence in their own decision-making abilities, so that someday, when they're grown, Jesus will be *their* choice and not just some habit they picked up from Mom and Dad.

For faith to be real, our kids need to own it—deeply, personally, and completely. It begins with Worry Woman backing off on the small choices. It begins with a watermelon.

### 3. Allow Dad to Be Dad—Relinquishing control to a coparent

Worry Woman's little control issue can cause her to question or orchestrate everything her kids do. This controlling attitude can easily trickle down to other people involved in caring for her children—namely, their father.

Oh yeah. Remember that guy?

Is your husband's parenting style different from yours? You're not alone. In a survey of women within my circle, 85 percent agreed that their parenting approach doesn't exactly gel with Dad's. My husband and I agree on family values and long-term goals for our kids, but when it comes to the smaller tasks and trials of raising children, we can be as different as apples and kumquats.

*Different does not mean wrong.*

In fact—at the risk of spurring you to hurl some of those rotten kumquats my way—might I suggest it's ever so possible that Dad's ideas might even be *better* than Mom's? Don't believe me? Take a little peek into the Kopitzke household on the day I first discovered Worry Woman's know-it-all side.

"Mom, where are my brown shoes?" My older daughter, four years old at the time, skipped into the kitchen where I was griddling pancakes for breakfast. I took one look at her and nearly flipped a flapjack to the floor.

"Did Daddy choose your outfit today?" Behold a stunning young redhead wearing camouflage overalls and a wrinkled pink T-shirt from the summer castoff pile—in winter. And are those *blue* socks I see? Pretty.

"Well, actually," she explained, "he let me pick it myself."

Ugh. It's not that the overalls were awful. I've never been a high-fashion mom, and I encourage creative expression.

But on this particular day, we were heading to a birthday party—an event at which other parents would be present; you know, parents who dressed their children in coordinated Old Navy outfits. I kind of wanted to be one of those parents.

This was my dilemma: Do I change my daughter's clothes and risk offending my husband, who had already approved the camouflage? (With the blue socks. Let's not forget the blue socks.) Or do I let it slide and simply appreciate that their dad was making a genuine effort to help?

I'd like to say I took the holy road. But would this be an interesting story if I'd done it right the first time?

Nooooo, I gently suggested to my preschool fashionista that maybe she'd like to wear the lovely purple dress hanging on her dresser. Her dad caught wind of this "suggestion" ("Daaaaad! Mom says I can't wear this!"), and let's just say it was not one of my finer family moments.

As the daytime-at-home parent, I have a system and a routine for getting through the day. My husband supports my role and my familiarity with our girls—what they eat, when they sleep, which library book is the latest favorite, and so on. He seeks my input and my guidance.

Shouldn't I also respect his?

Proverbs 1:8–9 says, *"Listen, my son, to your father's instruction and do not forsake your mother's teaching. They are a garland to grace your head and a chain to adorn your neck."*

This tells me that fathers and mothers are in the game together. For kids with two caring and well-intentioned parents in their lives, the wisdom from each is valuable. When we moms try to control child-rearing decisions and squelch a husband's input, we are effectively *denying our children a blessing their father was designed to impart.*

Yikes.

So the overalls weren't ideal, but they weren't the real issue, either. Once again, Worry Woman created a larger underlying problem. *Criticism.*

There came a point in my earlier mommy years when I was so rigid about my parenting routine that my husband confessed he felt like a visitor in his own home. Ladies, do not reduce your husband to the role of a visitor. He is not a spectator; he's the *head* of the household (Ephesians 5:22–23). He is just as important as you are in the raising of your children. In fact, sometimes he even trumps Mom.

Remember those pancakes I was flipping at the start of the scene? They used to go to waste, as my girls rarely took more than a few picky bites of their morning meal.

Until my husband announced a "standing breakfast" party.

He invited our daughters to park upright on low chairs at the kitchen counter, with their plates set in front of them. Would you believe those little stinkers ate the entire pancake that day? Now standing breakfast is a novelty in our house on special mornings when Mom is gone and Dad's in charge. So what if their clothes don't match and they're eating donuts instead of pancakes? My children are ridiculously happy and dearly loved by their amazing dad—therefore, I'm grateful.

## IS FEAR THE OPPOSITE OF FAITH?
Of all her evil powers, perhaps Worry Woman's most dangerous cunning is her ability to inflict spiritual amnesia on otherwise faith-filled moms. She whooped me *good* a couple years ago, on the final day of first grade.

I joined my daughter in her classroom to collect supplies

and snap a few farewell photos. It had been a fantastic school year, thanks to a loving and gifted teacher—a highly anticipated favorite among students and parents alike.

But *next year*. Ugh. We'd just caught wind that the upcoming second-grade teacher would be a new hire. An unknown.

Immediately the list of frets rolled through my mind.

*Will she be sensitive to my child's needs?*

*Will she load us down with homework?*

*Will she call me when my child has a stomachache?*

*Can I trust her?*

I lingered in the classroom chatting with the grandma of another first grader. "I hope next year is a good experience for the kids. I guess we'll find out, huh?"

"Oh, it will be." She nodded. "I have faith."

"You think so?" I crinkled my eyebrows.

"Of course I do." She looked at me straight on. "Just have faith."

*Hmmm.*

Just. Have. Faith.

Well, *duh*!

*Yeah*, have faith, Becky! Helloooo! Isn't that the definition of my life as a Christian? I live by faith, not by sight (2 Corinthians 5:7)! Yet still, after all I've learned, time and again I default to anxiety.

Worry Woman, you're so busted.

Have you heard the popular adage "Fear is the opposite of faith"? The first time I read that, it crushed me. Because the concept implies that if you have fear, then you must not have faith. Which I then translated to, if I'm afraid, then I must not be a Christian.

You know what the Bible says about that?

Hogwash.

*And I am convinced that nothing can ever separate us
from God's love. Neither death nor life, neither angels nor
demons, **neither our fears for today nor our worries about
tomorrow**—not even the powers of hell can separate us
from God's love. No power in the sky above or in the earth
below—indeed, nothing in all creation will ever be able to
separate us from the love of God that is revealed in Christ
Jesus our Lord. (Romans 8:38–39 NLT, emphasis added)*

Isn't that good news? Fear does not erase our faith.

But it does waste it.

When we fret, we choose to rely on ourselves instead of God.
And that's a really dumb choice. God knows more, cares more,
and sees so much more than we ever could. One of the benefits
of a personal relationship with God is His invitation for us to tap
into His sovereignty. Believe it. Trust it.

And we will not be disappointed.

*"And we know that God causes everything to work together for the
good of those who love God and are called according to his purpose for
them"* (Romans 8:28 NLT).

Imagine if we approached every situation with total confidence that it would turn out okay. Not just okay, but *good.* How
would that change our outlook? Our blood pressure? Our sanity?

Worry Woman could not survive under those conditions.

I left the first-grade classroom feeling humbled and relieved—
filled with a reclaimed sense of peace that God had everything
under control. And even if the second-grade teacher turned out to
be horrible (which did not happen), I believed God could use that
experience, too, somehow for our good.

We can't go wrong with God. *Duh.* So ladies, let's remember
who we are—women of faith, not of fear—and let's start living
like we mean it. Amen?

## OUR STRONGEST WEAPON AGAINST WORRY

There's one weapon against which Worry Woman has no defense. It's called trust.

Oh sure, it's easy to *say* we trust God. Every dollar bill in our diaper bags states that special claim. Applying trust to real life, however, can be the hardest thing we've ever done. My greatest test of trust thus far came in the form of an obstacle over which so many women since ancient times have clambered and wept.

Infertility.

I mentioned earlier that my husband and I had no trouble getting pregnant with our first daughter. We conceived the first month we tried, and I thank God every day for her—my joy, my teacher, the treasure of my heart.

We struggled in those first many months of learning to be parents, yes. Yet none of our challenges proved so overwhelming as to prevent us from filling what we perceived as empty space. We wanted another child. And we wanted one on our schedule.

So when it came time to calculate a precise two-year gap between our first and second baby, pragmatic Mom and Dad said, "Let's go!" and God said, *Wait.*

And wait.

And wait some more.

After six months, we consented to endure the tests. Our official diagnosis was no diagnosis at all—"secondary infertility," which is a catch-all term meaning the perplexing inability to conceive a subsequent child. Given my "advanced maternal age" (I was not yet thirty-five), my doctor had concerns about my egg supply, among other things. He gave us two years, maybe three, tops. So I found myself grieving not only the diminished hope of a second baby, but also the suddenly impossible dream of a third.

For six more months, we rode the fertility roller coaster. Many of you know it well and have traveled it much longer than I. Somewhere during the end of that tumultuous ride, I stopped begging God for another baby. Oh, I still wanted one, and God knew it. But I made the hard choice to put my trust into action and instead prayed along with Jesus in the Garden of Gethsemane, *"not as I will, but as you will"* (Matthew 26:39). I stopped focusing my prayers on what I wanted, and started thanking God for His plan. For protecting me from obstacles I couldn't see. For holding our family—however big or small—in His unshakable grasp.

I started thanking God for saying no. And crazy as that sounds, I really meant it.

When we reached the one-year point and it appeared our attempts had failed, I sought my husband in the backyard. He took one look at me, choked the lawn mower engine, and wrapped his strong arms around my back. I buried my face in his T-shirt and sobbed. We had already agreed we didn't want to pursue the next step of invasive medical interventions. If our first options for treatment didn't work, we would set our hopes aside and praise God no matter what.

A week later, I discovered I was pregnant after all.

I know the story doesn't end so neat and tidy for everyone. My heart aches for fellow moms who have endured great depths of fertility struggles, miscarriages, and infant loss. God's plan can be difficult to comprehend this side of heaven. That must be why He tells us not to depend on our logic.

*"Trust in the LORD with all your heart and lean not on your own understanding; in all your ways submit to him, and he will make your paths straight"* (Proverbs 3:5–6).

I've come to realize that infertility taught me to trust God in ways I hadn't before. In all my years of leaning on my own understanding, I was missing a deeper connection to the Giver of all good things. Yes, waiting on a baby was painful. But in the process I gained a stronger relationship with God, which is arguably the greater prize.

Our younger daughter arrived twelve days after her big sister's third birthday, and I've been hooked on that little critter since the very start. She drains my energy and warms my soul. Incidentally, baby number two was a much better sleeper than our firstborn. I like to say God threw us a bone the second time around—a reward for our patience and faith.

Does God have you in a waiting place? Are you wondering why He seems silent or stubborn or flat-out wrong? *Trust Him.* And when you do, Worry Woman has no place to dig her heels. Trust slays the villain every time.

*"Commit everything you do to the LORD. Trust him, and he will help you"* (Psalm 37:5 NLT).

# Chapter 4

# BUT THE NEIGHBORS ARE DOING IT

*Comparison is the death of joy.*
MARK TWAIN

**Dirty Villain No. 3:** Fence Hopper
**Evil Powers:** Comparison, envy, discontentment
**Kryptonite:** John 21:20–22; Galatians 6:4–5; 1 Corinthians 12:4–6; 1 Corinthians 12:27; Psalm 84:11; Matthew 6:25–33; Psalm 16:5–6; 2 Chronicles 7:14; Isaiah 26:3; Exodus 14:14; Psalm 139:23–24; Philippians 4:12–13; Romans 8:28; John 16:33; 2 Corinthians 4:16–18; Psalm 25:4–5

———

Mommy, look at my picture!" My four-year-old bounced on the floor outside her preschool classroom, jabbing an index finger toward the wall. "I made an apple tree! Do you see it?"

A row of painted art projects hung above the coat hooks. Brown trunks, swirls of green leaves, and fat red splotches representing, I presumed, the apples. With proud parent eyes, I examined the painting scrawled with my daughter's name, a mix of wobbly upper- and lowercase letters. "What a beautiful apple tree, sweetheart!" I reached to hug her. "You must've worked really hard on that picture!"

And then—I could not resist—I made a typical mom move.

I glanced again.

Just for ten seconds, I scrutinized the other kids' paintings.

Some of the trunks stood lopsided, some leaves appeared either overgrown or pruned. Some names were drawn neatly, some illegibly. A couple paintings looked more like a bush than a tree. I scolded myself for comparing, but the momma in me had to know—how did my child's talents stack up against the other preschoolers? Was she artistically on track? Did she comprehend the project? Had the other kids already mastered lowercase letters? Was she falling behind?

Could she be a genius?

Seriously. It was an *apple tree*. Not the SATs.

But we moms know how comparison creeps in even before birth. From pregnancy, we compare ourselves to other moms and our child to other children. We wonder why our prenatal butts grow wide while another lady carries nothing but a pelvic soccer ball. We wish our kids would sit still at the restaurant table like those mild-mannered children dipping french fries two booths over—without getting ketchup on their socks. We cheer for our student athletes at the volleyball game or the basketball tournament, involuntarily assessing our child's abilities in light of other players on the court.

Of course, comparison is not just reserved for parenting. It can seep into every aspect of our female lives. We compare ourselves to other women—our body shapes, our accomplishments, our husbands, our homes. We compare haircuts, shoe styles, front lawn hydrangeas, and Christmas cookie cutouts. *You use granulated sugar? Trust me, powdered is the way to go.*

Personally, I am guilty of comparing my laminate kitchen countertop to my friends' granite islands. Or even to someone else's newer laminate. It's practically a hobby for me.

Why do we do this?

Comparison is nearly as old as the human race, starting all the way back to the first family when Cain, eldest son of Adam and Eve, attacked and killed his brother Abel because Abel received greater favor from God (Genesis 4:1–8). The desire to compare ourselves to others is an inbred part of our sin nature.

No one is immune—not even the disciples.

> *Peter turned around and saw behind them the disciple Jesus loved—the one who had leaned over to Jesus during supper and asked, "Lord, who will betray you?" Peter asked Jesus, "What about him, Lord?"*
>
> *Jesus replied, "If I want him to remain alive until I return, what is that to you? As for you, follow me." (John 21:20–22 NLT)*

This passage comes from a scene toward the end of the Gospels in which the risen Jesus paid a visit to His disciples on the shoreline. Jesus had just given Peter some important instructions about his calling in life—to "feed my sheep"—but immediately, Peter took his eyes away from Jesus to look at John. And what did Peter say?

*"What about him?"*

Isn't that just like a human? The Lord of all creation had spoken straight to Peter's heart, yet Peter could not resist the temptation to let his focus stray onto other people and to compare his own lot in life to that of his friend.

In his sermon "Listening to Jesus beside the Sea," evangelical pastor and author Charles Swindoll paraphrased this episode.

> *Peter must have thought, "Who am I compared to Mr. Faithfulness (John)?" But Jesus clarified the issue. John was responsible for John. Peter was responsible for Peter. And each had only one command to heed: "Follow Me."*[1]

You are responsible for you. I am responsible for me. God calls us each to follow Him, which involves loving and encouraging one another, yes, but we must resist *comparing* ourselves to each other. When we compare, we're likely to draw one of two thorny conclusions: *I am better*, or *I am worse*. Neither is true according to God's design.

> *Make a careful exploration of who you are and the work you*
> *have been given, and then sink yourself into that. Don't be*
> *impressed with yourself. Don't compare yourself with others.*
> *Each of you must take responsibility for doing the creative*
> *best you can with your own life. (Galatians 6:4–5 MSG)*

Let's face it: we women are our own worst critics. We typically envision ourselves more *flawed* than *fabulous*, especially when held to the lamplight beside other supposedly amazing women. This act of comparison, whether deliberate or subtle, can then lead us to question or devalue God's call on our own lives. We turn our eyes to the proverbial "greener grass" across the fence until we dream of squishing our toes in it. This invites our third dirty villain—the Fence Hopper—to derail our focus. Sadly, the Fence Hopper's damage is progressive, because. . .

*Comparison leads to envy, which leads to discontentment.*

Do you see? Comparison is more than a trap; it's a tunnel. If we follow it through envy all the way to discontentment, not only will we suffer unnecessary heartache along the way, but we'll also inevitably discover the grass across that fence is not really greener after all. In fact, it might even be brown, muddy, or infested with thistles. It's best to stick with our own grass. Let's discover how—by examining in detail the Fence Hopper's three stages: comparison, envy, and discontentment.

## COMPARISON

Have you heard of a common debilitating condition infecting women today? It's called "shoulditis"—otherwise known as *I should do that* disease. I've got it. You probably do, too. Symptoms flare up under the most ordinary circumstances.

When my friend calls to say she's taking a Zumba class, I think of how long it's been since my sneakers hit the gym, and my own voice whispers in my head, *I should do that.*

When I scroll through Pinterest and see a dozen photos of cutesy craft projects other moms created with their children, I'm deflated. *I should do that.*

When my parenting magazine plugs a recipe for brownies using hidden carrot puree, I think of the Duncan Hines box stashed in my cupboard. *Carrots are way healthier. I should do that.*

Vacation plans. Extreme couponing. Colon-cleansing diets. Reading lists, scrapbooks, chore charts, and hand-sewn purses. Monkey-face pancakes, are you kidding me? *She* does it! I should do it, too!

But I can't do everything, can I?

Can you?

And that is the pain of shoulditis. It assumes we are supposed to be someone else—or a hundred someone elses. Our spirits inflame with an impossible itch to be as clever, resourceful, energetic, artsy, and self-disciplined as those *other women*.

Reality check. They can't do everything, either.

We all have our own *things*—our talents, interests, commitments, priorities. Yours aren't better than mine, and mine aren't better than yours. They're just *different*.

Why? Because God is fantastically creative, and He gave us each a unique blend of gifts. Trying to do it all is a waste of time. It's like saying God got it wrong. On the flip side, doing what He *created* us to do—that's worship.

*There are different kinds of spiritual gifts, but the same Spirit is the source of them all. There are different kinds of service, but we serve the same Lord. God works in different ways, but it is the same God who does the work in all of us. (1 Corinthians 12:4–6 NLT)*

So. Let's slap some salve on that shoulditis, shall we? (Say that five times fast.)

The antidote is: **I should *not* do that.**

When the neighbors rent a mega bounce house for their son's birthday party, I will tell myself, *I should* not *do that.* My children have winter birthdays, anyway. We can't fit a bounce house in the kitchen.

When my friend runs a half marathon—good for her! But *I should* not *do that.* Stroller walks are more my pace.

When that sweet lady in the church choir raves about her make-ahead freezer meals, *I definitely should* not *do that.* This momma prefers to spend Sunday afternoon playing Scrabble with the kids. I will grab some frozen chicken patties from the supermarket and call them dinner.

So let's all agree—you should do what you do, and I should do what I do, and together we will create a supportive, well-rounded community of women who love what they do and really *can* do it all—collectively.

*"All of you together are Christ's body, and each of you is a part of it"* (1 Corinthians 12:27 NLT).

## ENVY

Our backyard swing set bears a ladder to a lookout tower perched eight feet off the ground. It's handy for playing pirate ship in summer or sliding down snowdrifts in winter—but not so helpful for the neighbors' privacy. From inside the tower, we can see beyond our fence into the surrounding lots.

"Mom, I wish we lived in *that* house." My older daughter, age five at the time, cast wistful glances toward the neighbor's yard a few houses north.

"Why?" I wrinkled my eyebrows. "I thought you liked our house."

"Well, they have a pool and a picnic table."

*Ah. I see.* "But they don't have a sandbox," I reasoned. "Or swings. Or all your favorite toys inside." I wrapped my arms around my daughter's shoulders and turned her face toward mine. "Just because they have a pool doesn't mean that house is better. We belong here, in our house."

*Wise counsel, O Mommy Dear. Maybe you should take it yourself.*

How many times have I wished for someone else's stuff? *Their* finished basement, *their* three-car garage, *his* amazing talent, *her* silky hair.

And you, sweet mom friend—what are you spying across the fence wishing it were yours?

*Their* adventurous lifestyle.

*Their* healthy kids.

*Her* weekly housekeeper.

*His* obvious affection toward his wife.

You know what happens when we covet, don't you? The Fence Hopper pollutes our senses with her noxious Eau de Envy, that putrid toxin to the soul. And we start thinking our stuff isn't good enough. As if God doesn't know what we need. Or worse, *He's holding out on us.*

Now that is just ridiculous.

*"For the LORD God is a sun and shield; the LORD bestows favor and honor.* **No good thing does he withhold** *from those who walk up-rightly"* (Psalm 84:11 ESV, emphasis added).

The crazy thing is, there's probably somebody out there who's wishing for *your* stuff. Meanwhile, you're drooling over somebody *else's* stuff, which belongs to somebody who would finally be happy if only she could get her hands on somebody *else's* stuff—and on and on until the world is filled with ungrateful people.

It's madness, I tell you. Why can't we all just be happy with our own stuff?

The Fence Hopper forgets one simple truth: nobody has it all.

That *other* woman might be supermodel gorgeous on the outside but wrestling with heartache on the inside. That *other* husband's impressive job title might mean he hasn't been home to tuck his kids into bed for weeks. Your friend's new car has leather seats and a sunroof, sure, but she could be sweating the payments every month. Hardly anyone broadcasts the downside of their coveted stuff. If they did, who would want it?

Ultimately, I'd rather have my own problems than someone else's—because at least mine are familiar. If we really knew what went on in that bigger house or that supposedly perfect family, we might be relieved that it belongs to *them* and not *us*. In other words, we'd choose our own stuff.

At their core, envy and covetousness reveal a lack of confidence in God's plan and provision for our lives. *The Message* explains it this way:

> *"If you decide for God, living a life of God-worship, it*
> *follows that you don't fuss about what's on the table at*
> *mealtimes or whether the clothes in your closet are in fashion.*
> *There is far more to your life than the food you put in your*
> *stomach, more to your outer appearance than the clothes you*
> *hang on your body. Look at the birds, free and unfettered,*
> *not tied down to a job description, careless in the care of God.*
> *And you count far more to him than birds.*

*"Has anyone by fussing in front of the mirror ever gotten taller by so much as an inch? All this time and money wasted on fashion—do you think it makes that much difference? Instead of looking at the fashions, walk out into the fields and look at the wildflowers. They never primp or shop, but have you ever seen color and design quite like it? The ten best-dressed men and women in the country look shabby alongside them.*

*"If God gives such attention to the appearance of wildflowers—most of which are never even seen—don't you think he'll attend to you, take pride in you, do his best for you? What I'm trying to do here is to get you to relax, to not be so preoccupied with getting, so you can respond to God's giving. People who don't know God and the way he works fuss over these things, but you know both God and how he works. Steep your life in God-reality, God-initiative, God-provisions. Don't worry about missing out. You'll find all your everyday human concerns will be met." (Matthew 6:25–33)*

"Do you think that house has bunk beds, Mom?" Back in our lookout tower, my daughter pointed her telescope toward the neighbor's roof.

"Maybe." I shrugged. "But do you know what I'll bet it doesn't have?"

"What?" Her eyes grew wide.

"A supercool mom who bakes the yummiest oatmeal chocolate chip cookies in the universe. Want to go inside and make some?"

"Yeah! Let's go!"

If only the Fence Hopper were so easily deterred, eh, moms? Good news—she can be.

*"LORD, you alone are my portion and my cup; you make my lot*

secure. *The boundary lines have fallen for me in pleasant places; surely I have a delightful inheritance" (Psalm 16:5–6).*

What if our fence lines are established by God for our own *enjoyment* and *protection*? Doesn't that change how you look at your neighbor's lawn? God knows what you need. He knows His plans for your life. If you're a woman of faith, then those plans involve *your* family, *your* house, and *your* current circumstances— not someone else's.

That doesn't mean we shouldn't seek to grow, prosper, and pursue the goals God sets in our hearts. But if those pursuits are rooted in envy, we must concede they are not actually of God. And by hopping the fence to reach them, we enter dangerous territory, riddled with potential harm. On the other hand, if we return to the boundaries God designed for us, He promises healing and forgiveness.

*"If my people, who are called by my name, will humble themselves and pray and seek my face and turn from their wicked ways, then I will hear from heaven, and I will forgive their sin and will heal their land'" (2 Chronicles 7:14).*

So. You want to keep the Fence Hopper away? Remember these simple guidelines:

- My yard = boundaries and blessings designed just for me.
- Their yard = outside of God's plan for my life.

Do you want to live within God's plan or not? Seems like a dumb question, but when we invite the Fence Hopper into our homes, we're essentially answering no. Then, sadly, we set ourselves up to endure the greater havoc this dirty villain aims to wreak.

## DISCONTENTMENT

I recall one particular night when I truly saw the Fence Hopper for who she is—a liar and a thief. I had just tucked my girls into bed and, as was our routine in those days, I sat on the edge of my older daughter's mattress for a few minutes after lights out to pray. Stretching my legs across the width of her pink owl comforter, I watched dusk seep through the window blinds, shedding just enough fading daylight for my eyes to scan the familiar scenery.

In a bookcase on the wall, storybook spines lined the bottom shelf below stacks of cardboard puzzle boxes and early reader paperbacks. Stuffed animals, Velcro shoes, and a fraying jump rope lay strewn across the floor. In the corner, a dollhouse held mini furniture lovingly arranged for a plastic family of six. Above it all, hazy blue Dream Lite stars glowed on the ceiling.

I listened to the slow, steady breathing of two little girls drifting to sleep. And it occurred to me—this is as good as it gets.

I am blessed.

But. Rewind a few hours, and my mind raced with different thoughts. Grumpy thoughts.

Dirty dishes on the table. Deadlines on my desk. Bills to pay. Groceries to buy.

That leak in the ceiling. Chipped paint on the wall. Dust on the baseboards and juice in the carpet.

When can we build a new house? When can I afford a cleaning lady? Will my toddler ever ditch those Pull-Ups? How will I find time to bake cupcakes for the school picnic? And why are flights to Disney World so crazy expensive?

Is it summer yet?

*That's* when I'll be happy. When I have those things, carve that spare time, tie these loose ends, and tidy this clutter. *Then I'll be content. Then I can rest.*

Oh, really? That's exactly what the Fence Hopper wants us to believe. But sitting in my girls' room in the twilight, it suddenly occurred to me—I've got it all backward.

*Rest first.*

Take a break from running and complaining. Breathe in, breathe out. Pray. Then I can open my eyes and discover—*I'm already content.*

*"You will keep in perfect peace all who trust in you, all whose thoughts are fixed on you!" (Isaiah 26:3 NLT)*

A few years ago, a dear college friend told me she's living her dream. Four kids crowd her house, the budget is tight, noise and mess are constant, and yet she reminds herself daily that *this is what she wanted.*

When did I forget? Fifteen years ago, floundering through our early twenties, my friend and I both longed to be loved and settled. We wanted husbands, a mortgage, and our own laundry machines. We dreamed of ordinary family life, not because it's glamorous, but because it's meaningful.

And now I have it.

So what's the problem?

Worry. Distractions. Coveting. Complaints. Infections, all of them. They inflame a mother's perspective and steal her joy. But I've discovered a cure.

## STILLNESS

Try it. Sit still for a minute—I mean really *park* your harried self, just for a moment—and take a look around. What do you see?

I see LEGOs scattered where my socks are sure to step. I see half-empty ice-cream bowls stuck to the carpet, waiting for a hitch to the dishwasher. I see homework logs to sign and overdue library books stacked in the corner behind a heap of jackets and shoes and backpacks.

This is the picture of my humble existence. And if I view it in light of God's presence, I will see with crystal clarity—*I'm already living the life I always wanted.* It might be messy, yes. Cluttered, hectic, and imperfect, absolutely. But it's beautiful. And it's mine.

It's *yours.* Do you see it?

"'The LORD will fight for you; you need only to be still'" *(Exodus 14:14).*

Ladies, we don't need to focus ahead to that elusive house upgrade or Florida vacation. We are in the center of God's blessings right here, right now. Who knew they'd smell like peanut butter and Pull-Ups, right? Sometimes I think we expect God to show up all shiny and clean. But the truth is He's in the muck with us every day. We just have to focus our hearts to find Him.

So will you join me? Let's shut off our racing brains for a minute, wrestle that old Fence Hopper to the ground, and take a good look around. I hope you'll see what I see.

*Contentment* is within our grasp.

We're already blessed.

## GODLY VERSUS WORLDLY DISCONTENTMENT

What does it really mean to be content? I'll tell you what it does *not* mean. Contentment is not apathy or idleness. It's not an absence of goals, ambitions, or personal drive to excel. God wants us to pursue excellence in the work we do for our families, jobs, homes, and ministries, and He commands us to persevere. A contented Christian works hard and prays even harder.

True contentment means putting God in charge and embracing His plans for your life, even when they're different from your own. So you wanted six children and God gave you two. Do you trust Him? You imagined cake and ice cream for every birthday party, but your child is allergic to wheat and dairy. Do you know God makes no mistakes? And yes, maybe you dreamed of living Pacific beachside, but God landed your family in Wisconsin. I feel your pain, sister. Yet do you truly believe He knows what's best for your life? And can you stop playing tug-of-war with Him long enough to count your blessings?

That is godly contentment. It's a hard-fought peace.

On the flip side, in order to fully understand *discontentment*, we need to examine its two sources: God and the world. The truth is, not all discontentment is bad. Sometimes it actually comes from God. This is called godly discontentment, and God uses it to motivate, move, and grow us according to His plan.

My husband recently experienced a season of godly discontentment with his job, in which it became clear to us that God was nudging him out of his tenured role into a new, riskier career path. The process was painful at times, exciting at others, and some days we just looked at each other and thought, *Are we crazy?* Yet we trusted that if the source of discontent was indeed the Lord, then we could rely on Him to *guide* and *provide*. And He did.

Worldly discontentment, however, is not from God. It's a rotten gift from the Fence Hopper, like dog droppings dumped in your yard. Worldly discontentment is rooted in envy, selfishness, greed, worry, complaining, and other unlovely sins, and it's not aligned with God's will for our lives. We may all wrestle with worldly discontentment from time to time. The trick is to recognize it when it comes. How? Ask yourself these questions:

- Am I comparing my situation to someone else's?
- Am I counting my blessings or losing sight of them?
- Am I engaging in any obvious sin (greed, coveting, selfishness)?

Then pray for God to reveal the source of your discontent.

*"Search me, God, and know my heart; test me and know my anxious thoughts. See if there is any offensive way in me, and lead me in the way everlasting" (Psalm 139:23–24).*

## CONTENTMENT IS AN ACQUIRED SKILL

The Fence Hopper tries to convince us that happiness is always just one step away. If only we could gain *this* or *that* particular desire beyond our reach, then life would be fulfilled at last! Right?

Wrong.

Contentment is not *gained*. It's *learned*.

In the final chapter of Philippians, the apostle Paul wrote to the church in Philippi:

*I know what it is to be in need, and I know what it is to have plenty. I have learned the secret of being content in any and every situation, whether well fed or hungry, whether living in plenty or in want. I can do all this through him who gives me strength. (Philippians 4:12–13)*

Paul *learned* the secret of being content. And what is that secret? Jesus. "I can do all this through him who gives me strength" (verse 13).

It's easy to love Jesus when life is going well, isn't it? When your marriage is happy, your kids are healthy, the money keeps rolling in, and everybody's getting straight A's, well, God is good! Praise Him for His blessings!

But what about those times when life isn't feeling so hot? Maybe you're in conflict with your husband or the kids are out of control. You're making too many trips to the doctor. Finances are stressful, and dreams are derailed. Any number of hardships and disappointments can cause us to question God's goodness.

But that does not change the fact that *He is still good*—and at every moment, in ways we cannot possibly fathom, God is working out the details of our lives for good reason and good results.

*"And we know that in all things God works for the good of those who love him, who have been called according to his purpose" (Romans 8:28).*

Do you know where Paul was when he wrote his letter to the Philippians? He was under house arrest in Rome, probably chained to a Roman guard twenty-four hours a day. He could receive visitors, but under constant watch Paul was essentially powerless to spread the good news of Jesus in the manner he desired—as a free man. Evangelical pastor and author Dr. Charles Stanley put it this way:

> *Under such circumstances, Paul might have been tempted to cry out to heaven for release. After all, God had called him to preach, to disciple believers, and to reach the Gentiles. But he was stuck in Rome, unable to plant new churches or visit those whom he was nurturing by letter. Beside being unjust, the imprisonment was keeping him from important work. Surely, if anyone had a right to gripe, it was Paul, who'd endured persecution, shipwreck, and beatings for the gospel. Yet he never once complained. His letter to the church at Philippi is filled with rejoicing, as focusing on God let him live above his circumstances (Philippians 4:8).*
>
> *The more we talk and complain about a situation, the worse it looks, until the problem looms larger in our mind than our faith does. Conversely, carrying challenges straight to God keeps matters in perspective. The Lord is bigger than any hardship. On His strength, we rise above the difficulty.[2]*

The Fence Hopper says, *God doesn't want what's best for you. You need to go find it somewhere else.* But the woman of God holds fast to the words of Jesus, who said, *"In this world you will have trouble. But take heart! I have overcome the world" (John 16:33)*.

At the core of true contentment is an unshakable assurance of two facts: God will provide what is best, and this world is not all there is for us. As believers, we must remember that nothing on this earth can separate us from God's promise of heaven. Beyond our current circumstances, no matter how miserable a day, a week, or year after year may seem, our ultimate reward is infinitely greater than any pain or discouragement we suffer meanwhile.

> *Therefore we do not lose heart. Though outwardly we are wasting away, yet inwardly we are being renewed day by day. For our light and momentary troubles are achieving for us an eternal glory that far outweighs them all. So we fix our eyes not on what is seen, but on what is unseen, since what is seen is temporary, but what is unseen is eternal. (2 Corinthians 4:16–18)*

If Paul could learn to be content in prison, I think I can learn to be content with my laminate countertops. What about you? What triggers the Fence Hopper to show up at your door? Can you give it up to God today? Because if contentment can be *learned*, then it can also be *taught*. And God is one amazing Teacher.

*"Show me your ways, LORD, teach me your paths. Guide me in your truth and teach me, for you are God my Savior, and my hope is in you all day long" (Psalm 25:4–5)*.

# Chapter 5

## JUST A MINUTE!

*You'll miss the best things if you keep your eyes shut.*
Dr. Seuss

**Dirty Villain No. 4:** Calendar Queen
**Evil Powers:** Overscheduled, hurried, distracted, preoccupied
**Kryptonite:** Psalm 39:6–7; Proverbs 14:26; Mark 10:13–16;
Ecclesiastes 3:1–7; John 17:4; Micah 6:8; Ephesians 2:10;
Proverbs 16:9; Proverbs 31:27; Psalm 139:16; 2 Corinthians
5:7; Romans 12:2; Luke 10:38–42; Psalm 46:10; John 6:14–
15; John 15:4–5; Joshua 24:15

---

My husband and I enjoy surprising our girls occasionally with a trip to the local frozen yogurt bar. It's the kind of heavenly smorgasbord where dozens of self-serve flavors and toppings are limited only by your appetite—and your wallet. At forty-five cents per ounce, my cup usually tops five dollars or more. What can I say, cookie dough is bulky.

On one of these memorable outings, I discovered there's a system to proper fro-yo family fun. Mothers, before you create your own dessert, you must first supervise your hungry children. Because this is what happens when you don't.

"Mom, I think I'm full." My seven-year-old grimaced, stuck out her tongue, and shoved her cardboard cup across the table.

"How was your concoction?" I peeked inside her cup, still half full of candy bits floating in a melted pool of goo. "Wowsers, what did you put in this thing?"

"Just some good stuff."

"What yogurt flavors did you have?"

"Um, I got cake batter, pink lemonade, and rocky road."

"Yum." I gagged. "And I see some Skittles in there."

"And peanuts, cookie dough"—she counted off her selected toppings one finger at a time— "M&M's, Heath bar, Butterfinger, rock candy, Nerds, sprinkles, blackberries. . ."

"Gummy bears," my husband reminded her.

"Oh yeah, gummy bears and whipped cream!" She flashed a grin then wrinkled her nose and slid back in her chair. "I have a tummy ache."

No kidding. Hey, there's nothing wrong with cake batter yogurt or gummy bears in general. On their own, they're quite tasty, I'm sure. But pile too many good things on top of one another, and you have a recipe for indigestion.

Every sensible mom knows this about sundaes.

But what about our *weekdays*?

Take one glance at my calendar and you'll see plenty of "good" things. Bible study, book club, praise band, freelance work, conferences, exercise class, coffee dates, prayer groups, speaking engagements, dinner with friends, playdates for the kids, and the constant carpooling to tennis lessons, tumbling class, ballet, and school. Individually, such excellent pursuits! But toppled into a heap of a day or a week or a year, this kind of to-do list can settle like a rock in my gut.

Literally.

Stress for me manifests as stomachaches. When my schedule trips a threshold, I can measure my diminishing mental and physical margin by the number of Rolaids I reach for at bedtime. So just as my daughter swallowed too many treats at once, trying to consume too many *activities* at one time can also create a serious case of belly rot.

Or worse.

*"We are merely moving shadows, and all our busy rushing ends in nothing. We heap up wealth, not knowing who will spend it. And so, Lord, where do I put my hope? My hope is in you"* (Psalm 39:6–7 NLT).

Our next dirty villain is a very busy woman. She is characteristically preoccupied with her to-do list, her smartphone, her personal agenda, and any clock in sight. I call her the Calendar Queen—because this poor gal really believes she holds court over her ridiculously packed schedule.

Truth is? Her schedule controls *her*.

Let's take a thorough and sobering look at what happens when the Calendar Queen draws us away from our two greatest priorities—our family and God. Then we'll learn how to block this dirty villain's number and cut her off for good—by accepting God's amazing invitation *to be more by doing less*.

## IF YOU GIVE A MOM A MINUTE

I have a confession to make. I steal from my children. Shocking, right? But hey, guess what. You probably steal from your children, too.

Oh, the loot is nothing tangible. I mean, I don't swipe dollars from their piggy banks or cookies off their lunch plates. And if that cute pair of earrings you're wearing came from your daughter's jewelry box this morning, well, you won't see me pointing fingers.

What I'm talking about is more valuable. You and I, we steal *time*. Under the influence of the Calendar Queen, bit by bit we moms snatch precious time with our children—in increments of *just a minute*.

"Mom, can I please have a cup of juice with my breakfast?" my older daughter piped up from the dining table while I closed cereal box flaps and returned peanut butter to the cupboard.

"Sure, sweetheart, just give me a minute."

"Come see my picture, Momma! I colored it for you!" Little sister shrieked from her chair, where she sat grasping a handful of crayons.

"Wonderful!" I smiled. "I'll be there in a minute."

"Mom, I need your help. I can't pull the cap off my glue stick." My older daughter frowned. I glanced up briefly at both girls before wrapping a twist tie around a bread bag.

"Okay, just a minute."

"Will you read me this book, Momma? Please?" The little one pattered toward me with a favorite story in her hands.

*Just a minute, girls*—I need to finish emptying the dishwasher. While stacking plates, I noticed crumbs scattered around the toaster, so I wiped the counter. When I hung the dishcloth on the faucet, I saw the sink needed scrubbing, which reminded me we were almost out of paper towels, so I sat down to write the shopping list. Shopping made me think about the checkbook, so I flipped open my laptop and paid a few bills online. And since I was already at the computer, I figured I might as well send a quick e-mail to my sister.

"Mom? Did you forget about my juice?"

Oops.

If you give a mom a minute—she'll take twenty. Then minutes add up to hours, and hours add up to *days* spent investing in our own preoccupations rather than our children.

Should a mom be her child's slave? No. That is not at all what I'm suggesting. We mothers do have responsibilities to attend to, and delayed gratification can teach young ones patience and selflessness.

But I'm not talking about unreasonable demands here. When our kids ask for juice or books, they're really asking for something else.

They want *us.*

Our attention. Our affirmation. Our love. They want to feel safe.

We are their safe place.

*"Those who fear the L*ORD *are secure; he will be a refuge for their children"* (Proverbs 14:26 NLT).

How many times a day do you say, "Just a minute"? For me, the answer used to be *too many.* It was once my default reply. But not anymore. When I recognized this mantra as the voice of the evil Calendar Queen, I saw how she was cheating me out of a closer relationship with my children. So I became determined to switch it around. Now, instead of *stealing* minutes, I *grant* them.

*Yes, I will bring you that juice—because it's only going to cost me a minute.*

*Sure, I can help with that glue stick. It'll interrupt my dishes for just a little minute.*

*I'd love to read that book. My to-do list can pause a minute—or twenty—because that's all it really takes to make you feel important.*

Think this sounds impossible, or even unnecessary? Then the Calendar Queen is whispering lies in your face. It doesn't matter how crazy busy or important you are—nobody is busier than God. And even He gladly granted minutes to His children.

> *People were bringing little children to Jesus for him to place his hands on them, but the disciples rebuked them. When Jesus saw this, he was indignant. He said to them, "Let the little children come to me, and do not hinder them, for the kingdom of God belongs to such as these." . . . . And he took the children in his arms, placed his hands on them and blessed them. (Mark 10:13–14, 16)*

In this particular passage, Jesus was at the height of His ministry, teaching crowds of people in Judea about the kingdom of God. A big job, right? With so much important work to be done, His disciples took it upon themselves to protect Jesus from petty interruptions from children.

But what did Jesus do? Did He thank them for their help? No way. According to scripture, Jesus was *indignant*. The Greek word for "indignant" here is *aganakteo*, which means "much grief." Jesus was *grieved* to see His disciples shooing away the children. This was a serious offense in His eyes. So Jesus set the disciples straight. *These children are not pestering me. My kingdom is their kingdom. By all means, let them come to me.* And He took the time to hold these precious babes in His arms and bless them.

Can we do the same for our own children? They need our attention, and Jesus says they ought to have it. Your kingdom is their kingdom, too. Therefore, more often than we allow, everything else on our schedules can wait *just a minute.*

## THE TROUBLE WITH TO-DO

If the first step to slapping down the Calendar Queen is reclaiming minutes, then the next step is reclaiming days, weeks, months, and years—in other words, long-term vision. I'm talking about the classic battle between *urgent* and *important*.

When my older daughter was four, she loved to play a game called "checklist." I would write a series of tasks on her favorite monkey-face-shaped notebook, and she would draw a check mark next to each completed assignment.

- ✓ Draw a flower.
- ✓ Spell your name.
- ✓ Hop five times.
- ✓ Sing the ABCs.

She got this idea from her mother, of course. I'm a check-list addict. I keep lists for everything—groceries, housekeeping, Christmas gifts, party plans. My own trusty notebook sits on our kitchen countertop, catching random assignments for each day.

- ✓ Wash the sheets.
- ✓ Sign permission slip.
- ✓ Thaw hamburger.
- ✓ Call Mom.

What does this say about me? I'm organized. I'm methodical. Or, more likely, I'm flaky enough to forget things if I don't write them down. Lists help me spew thoughts onto paper instead of cramming them inside my daydreaming, overanalytical brain. For me, checklists are a form of mental freedom.

But they're also a crutch.

I like to cross things off the list. So I spend a lot of time chasing immediate to-dos instead of long-term, important stuff.

- ✓ I did the laundry, but I let my child's *High Five* magazines pile up, unread.

- ✓ I scoured Pinterest for the perfect birthday cake, but I haven't yet updated our photo books with last year's party pictures.

- ✓ I paid the bills, but I've been meaning for half a year now to create a chore chart designed to teach our children fiscal responsibility. They have yet to earn a single quarter—because I still haven't made the chart.

Bills have a due date. Life lessons do not. So the urgent crowds out the important, day in and day out, until my menial tasks are accounted for but I've lost opportunities to train my children, to invest in my marriage, and to improve my own well-being.

What if my checklist looked like this?

✓ Take a romantic weekend getaway to a log cabin.
✓ Train for a 5K.
✓ Read classic novels to my children at bedtime.

These are projects I've been meaning to do for a long time. But they get shoved to the bottom of the list because they're not immediately attainable. The pots have to get scrubbed, the preschool snack has to be divided into baggies, and somebody has to run to the store to buy more milk. So those are the tasks I tackle first. Until they're the only tasks I tackle at all.

God has a checklist, too. Did you know that?

*"There is a time for everything, and a season for every activity under the heavens. . .a time to search and a time to give up, a time to keep and a time to throw away, a time to tear and a time to mend, a time to be silent and a time to speak" (Ecclesiastes 3:1, 6–7).*

✓ search
✓ give up
✓ keep
✓ throw away
✓ tear
✓ mend
✓ be silent
✓ speak

Every pair of tasks seems at odds, but God gives them equal weight. Today, search. Tomorrow, give up. By all means, keep. But don't neglect to throw away.

Do you see the beauty of the pattern? It's not about choosing between this and that, urgent or important. *There is time to do both*. The Calendar Queen would convince us to tip our agenda too heavily to one side.

Don't listen to her.

What can you postpone this week in order to focus some time on what matters for the long haul? *There is a time for everything*. Let's give our calendars a chance to prove it.

- ✓ Do not vacuum.
- ✓ Hop on the treadmill.

- ✓ Log off Facebook.
- ✓ Call an old friend.

- ✓ Skip the casserole prep.
- ✓ Order pizza and play board games with the kids.
- ✓ See what God does!

## STOP FOLDING YOUR UNDERWEAR

Do you ever complain, *There just aren't enough hours in the day*? I used to do that, too. Until I realized most of the stuff taxing my schedule was my own darn fault.

"Can I fold this laundry?" Our babysitter, a retired teacher in her sixties, lovely woman, pointed to a basket of my daughters' clothes and offered her motherly help.

"Oh my goodness." I blushed at the piles of unfinished housework sitting stark naked on the living room floor. "I'm so sorry I left these baskets here for you to trip over. I just didn't get to them last night."

"Oh now"—she dismissed my jabber with a flick of her

wrist—"you know I was a young mom once, too. It's the least I can do." She grabbed a pair of princess undies, checked the label, and flattened them into a stack of size 4s.

*Flattened.* Unfolded. Took her 0.3 seconds.

"You don't fold the underwear?" I asked—not so much a question, but a statement of bewilderment. Epiphany. Awe.

"No." She smiled then crinkled her nose. "Do you?"

"Yes."

"Why?"

*Uhhhhh.*

"I. . .don't. . .know."

Why *do* I fold the underwear? I mean, it's not like anybody ever looks in our skivvy drawers but us. And must I see a tidy arrangement of britches staring back at me?

No. Not as much as I'd prefer to cut my laundry folding time in half.

*Hmmm.*

Think about it. What else do we do—out of habit or compulsion or ignorance, even—that sucks up our precious time *unnecessarily*? Maybe you don't fold your underwear, but do you alphabetize your spices? Dust behind the sofa? Check e-mail ten times a day when once or twice will do?

It's fair to ask the question.

Why?

In her book *Lies Women Believe*, author Nancy Leigh DeMoss explains that God gave us exactly twenty-four hours in a day, and if we can't accomplish everything on our to-do lists within His parameters, then we're probably adding our own agenda items to God's plan.

*In fact, the Lord Jesus Himself was given only a few short years on earth to accomplish the entire plan of redemption.*

*Talk about a long "to do" list! Yet, at the end of His life, Jesus was able to lift His eyes to His Father and say, "I have glorified thee on the earth: I have finished the work which thou gavest me to do" (John 17:4 KJV).*[1]

Did you catch that? The work *which thou [God] gavest me to do.* The key to preventing the Calendar Queen from oversaturating and misguiding our schedules is *discernment*—knowing the difference between what God asks of us, and what we demand of ourselves.

Honestly? I'm pretty sure God never told me to fold the underwear. So of all the choices we have regarding how to spend a day, what *does* God ask us to do?

Walk with Him.

*"He has shown you, O mortal, what is good. And what does the LORD require of you? To act justly and to love mercy and to walk humbly with your God" (Micah 6:8).*

What does it mean to walk with God? Well, imagine taking a long walk with a dear friend. You talk, you laugh, you cry. You keep in step with one another along the same path. Walking with God involves this same type of companionship, only it's not a one-time excursion but a lifelong journey. God determines the route and sets the pace—that's the "walk *humbly*" part—and He invites you to share your heart with him even as you trek into puddles and trip over sidewalk cracks. He's a true friend and trustworthy guide.

The longer we walk with God, the better we get to know Him, and the more we'll discover what He wants for us. This faith journey will look different for everyone. But your walk and my walk have this in common—each path is mapped out by a flawless, loving, intentional God.

*For we are God's handiwork, created in Christ Jesus to do good works, which God prepared in advance for us to do" (Ephesians 2:10).*

Do you see? In order to choose what's *important* over what's *urgent*—what God deems *best* over what's merely *good* or popular or (*hello, underwear!*) ridiculous—busy moms must start giving up some tasks, especially the ones that don't matter. And if you're the kind of gal who has a hard time saying no, think of it this way. Every "no" to a superfluous time stealer is a "yes" to your family, your sanity, and God.

## INTERRUPTIONS—FRIENDS OR FOES?

"Mom, I love these french fries!" My firstborn, age four at the time, opened wide and popped another fry in her mouth. We were eating dinner at a neighborhood burger joint, complete with old-fashioned milkshakes and my favorite people seated around the table. It was the stuff memories are made of.

Bad memories.

Halfway through dinner, my one-year-old coughed and threw up all over my shirt.

"Where did *that* come from?!" I sat with my eyes bulging, helpless and stunned while the baby heaved in my arms. My husband scrambled for napkins, and—as if we needed more attention drawn to our appetizing scene—our four-year-old started bawling.

"Mom, I don't like my fries anymore!" she wailed. "That wasn't supposed to happen!"

Tell me about it.

As moms, our days are defined by interruptions. Sick kids, playground injuries, tantrums, scary dreams. We can't schedule them into convenient time slots, so the Calendar Queen gets peeved. She stews in the pit between what *is* and what *should have been*, grumbling all the while—*this is* not *how today was supposed to go!*

But who are we to decide that?

*"In their hearts humans plan their course, but the LORD establishes their steps"* (Proverbs 16:9).

Planning is wise, to a point. The Bible says the wife of noble character *"watches over the affairs of her household and does not eat the bread of idleness"* (Proverbs 31:27). God wires many of us to be organized, punctual, and efficient, which are admirable traits indeed.

Yet we must be careful not to presume that our plans are more sensible than God's.

He is the all-knowing keeper of time. Surely He has your calendar in the palm of His hand, because His Word says, *"all the days ordained for me were written in your book before one of them came to be"* (Psalm 139:16). Therefore, what to us looks like an interruption, is to God simply staying the course.

The question is, do you trust His course?

Ultimately, interruptions—whether big or small—are a test of our faith in God. Yes, I know it's maddening when a potty accident derails a playdate, or a fever thwarts your long-awaited vacation. But God always knows something we don't know. His plans are always better calculated than ours, and He protects us from countless invisible dangers every single day. That is why, as Christians, we walk by faith and not by sight (2 Corinthians 5:7).

## BUSY IS NOT BETTER

Women today are blessed with a bounty of opportunities. I'm grateful for modern equality and the potential it allows not only me, but also my daughters. Trouble comes, though, when we stand at that proverbial frozen yogurt bar and fill our cups with too many opportunities at once.

Romans 12:2 says, *"Do not conform to the pattern of this world, but be transformed by the renewing of your mind. Then you will be able to test and approve what God's will is—his good, pleasing and perfect will."*

The world tells us we ought to stuff ourselves, that it's no longer enough to care for our family's basic needs. We must enrich every moment with technology, extracurricular activities, volunteering, social commitments, work, and personal development. Why? Because we can! It's all available to us now, and so we buy into the Calendar Queen's lie that if we don't keep up then we must be missing out—or worse, be lazy.

But what does God say?

> *As Jesus and his disciples were on their way, he came to a village where a woman named Martha opened her home to him. She had a sister called Mary, who sat at the Lord's feet listening to what he said. But Martha was distracted by all the preparations that had to be made. She came to him and asked, "Lord, don't you care that my sister has left me to do the work by myself? Tell her to help me!"*
>
> *"Martha, Martha," the Lord answered, "you are worried and upset about many things, but few things are needed—or indeed only one. Mary has chosen what is better, and it will not be taken away from her." (Luke 10:38–42)*

Are you "worried and upset about many things"? Is your to-do list taking over your desire for God Himself? No wonder the Bible urges us, *don't conform to that lifestyle.* Busy is not better. More productive does not mean more purposeful, more accomplished, or more accepted. Instead, God says, "Be still, and know that I am God" (Psalm 46:10). When we do this, we'll discover that the Lord is wonderfully countercultural. And that might be the best news a busy mom needs to hear.

## FIND YOUR MOUNTAIN

Honestly, when I hear the words *be still*, my nerves start buzzing involuntarily. A woman who is wired to "do" (as the Calendar Queen is) can "be still" about as long as she can go without blinking—thirty seconds, tops. At times it can seem nearly impossible to break away from a pressing schedule to be still with God. Yet our greatest example of this practice comes from someone whose job was far more demanding than ours—Jesus Himself.

In the famous "loaves and fishes" story in the Gospel of John, Jesus had just transformed a meager basket of food into a feast for five thousand people:

> *After the people saw the sign Jesus performed, they began to say, "Surely this is the Prophet who is to come into the world." Jesus, knowing that they intended to come and make him king by force, withdrew again to a mountain by himself. (John 6:14–15)*

On several occasions in the Gospels, Jesus leaves a bustling scene in order to go to a solitary place to pray. Here is a man who has every reason to keep healing, keep feeding, and keep teaching the throngs of people at His feet, but He knows when to step away and *serve* God by *seeking* God. More so, He knew when other people's expectations of Him were different from what God expected of Him. To be crowned king of the nation by force or rebellion? Nope, not God's plan. So Jesus did what we also ought to do under those circumstances. Nothing. He withdrew to the mountain—a quiet space to meet with God.

Can you tell when demands on your time and talents are overwhelming or outside of God's will for you? Resist the wrong yes. Retreat and pray. Counterproductive as that may seem, it's actually the smartest move you can make.

## WHEN YOUR QUIET TIME IS ANYTHING BUT QUIET

Early in my mommy career, I'd wilt into an armchair every evening, completely wiped out from a full day of diaper changing, toddler chasing, laundry sorting, and colicky baby bouncing. My husband would appear through the mental fog, presumably expecting either sex or popcorn. I'd buy some time and suggest we watch *Cupcake Wars*. Then it would hit me.

*Noooooooooo! I haven't touched my Bible today! How could I let that slide again?* My wasted brain wrestled with how to spend those precious thirty minutes of "me" time. *Bible, TV. Bible, TV.* I'm ashamed to admit it wasn't an automatic decision.

Has that ever happened to you? The demands of family and work and *life* command every minute of the day—and every ounce of energy we can muster. Sadly, it's easy to crowd God out of the calendar.

As if He's just another item on the to-do list.

*"Remain in me, as I also remain in you. No branch can bear fruit by itself; it must remain in the vine. Neither can you bear fruit unless you remain in me. I am the vine; you are the branches. If you remain in me and I in you, you will bear much fruit; apart from me you can do nothing."*
*(John 15:4–5)*

Did you catch that? *Apart from me you can do nothing.* All our housekeeping, child rearing, errands, work—it amounts to zero without Jesus. He's our *sustenance*, ladies. When we let ourselves slip out of the vine, we become withered branches, useless and barren. No wonder we're drained.

In a perfect world, this is exactly when we would retreat to our mountain—that precious quiet place to meet with God. Many women go there at the crack of dawn because it's the only peaceful hour in the house. But let's be real. During certain seasons of life, a solid block of quiet is crazy impossible to carve. Ask any woman who's jolted awake three times a night by a hungry baby—5:00 a.m. isn't quiet time; it's the shift change.

Out of necessity, I learned long ago to invite God into my not-so-quiet day. It isn't pretty, but it works. Here's how.

First, start each morning acknowledging God, praying while you stretch your aching limbs out of bed. *Lord, thank You for another day with my children. Help me to honor You with the way I treat my family today.*

Then crack open your Bible while the kids play at your feet. While you're idling in the school carpool line, nursing your baby, or sitting on the soccer sidelines waiting for the game to start—wherever you are, invite God to join you. I used to read my Bible while I sat on my toddler's bed as she drifted off to nap. Or I'd sneak a few verses from Proverbs while the family watched TV. I told Bible stories to my kids at bedtime, and still do. From the beginning, I learned to talk *to* and *about* Jesus in daily conversation, keeping Him close to my heart as I went about the responsibilities He gave me.

Maybe it's not ideal, the constant activity, the noise. It's like inviting God for coffee at McDonald's Playland. But it's time with God nonetheless.

Besides, imagine if we moms reserved all our time with God for the moments when our kids are sleeping or absent. They'd never get to see our faith relationship in action. When we read the Bible in front of our children, when we pray with them, when we point to God in ordinary scenery, we're remaining in the Vine—and we're teaching our kids that in this house, God is top priority.

"*But as for me and my household, we will serve the* Lord." (Joshua 24:15).

# Chapter 6

## AM I THE MAID AROUND HERE?

*Housework is what a woman does that*
*nobody notices unless she hasn't done it.*
EVAN ESAR

**Dirty Villain No. 5:** The Maid
**Evil Powers:** Neat-freak tendencies, house neglect
**Kryptonite:** John 1:14; Mark 8:18; Proverbs 31:17; Luke 9:1–2;
Matthew 4:23–25; Matthew 5:1–2, 5; Colossians 3:23–24;
Romans 12:9–13

———

It was eight o'clock on a typical Sunday evening. I hauled the last basket of clean laundry from the basement and dropped it with a thud onto the family room carpet. Then I stared at it for a good thirty seconds before I heaved a sigh, grabbed a sock, and dug for its match.

In the last fourteen hours, I'd wrestled little arms and feet into church clothes, play clothes, the bathtub, and bed; cooked and cleaned up after three meals, two snacks, and four sticky ice-cream cones; washed, dried, folded, and put away five loads of laundry; trucked to the grocery store, the gas station, the Dollar Store, and Target; and mediated at least a dozen sibling squabbles while sorting Nerf darts and picking chunks of dried Play-Doh off the kitchen floor.

This was my Sabbath day.

Funny—it looked a lot different from my husband's.

Because while I busted my housewife behind, he lounged

on the couch watching baseball. Reading the newspaper. Eating chips and checking e-mail.

And as I reached for the very last pair of underwear in the bottom of the laundry basket, he peeled his eyes from the TV, glanced at me, and said, "Do you need any help?"

Do. I. Need. HELP? *Why, yes, husband. Thanks for asking. I do need some help, actually. I need help understanding why you get to nap in a chair while I chop onions for your dinner. And then I need everyone in this family to stop wearing underwear so that I. . .don't. . . have. . .to. . .wash it anymoooooore!*

Recognize this lady? She's not the wife or the mom. She's the Maid. And she isn't just worn out—she's steaming mad.

Because she works hard for her family and feels underpaid. She wants a break but doesn't take one—even when everyone else does—because hey, somebody has to feed the people and fold their clothes. Yet the poor old gal is fed up with stacking T-shirts and spreading jelly while the rest of the family plays kickball in the kitchen. *Really? You didn't see that jug of chocolate milk on the table when you hurled the ball straight for it? Get me a mop. And go to your room.*

The Maid tends to infiltrate my attitude on a regular basis— particularly anytime there are chores to be done. Which we moms know is every hour of every day. Housework is an un- avoidable part of family life, because where humans dwell, mess will follow. How we cope with it, well, that's a touchy subject.

Personally, I'm a recovering neat freak. Recovering a little too well, I confess. In the last eight years of parenting, I've swung from one extreme to the other—from spotless to care- less. When my first daughter was born and the exhausting de- mands of infant care seized me, I quickly discovered I could maintain either my home or my sanity, so I reluctantly chose my sanity. Little by little I let go of certain housekeeping standards until my second daughter arrived, at which point I waved a white flag at the mess and decided there would be plenty of time to vacuum when the kids went off to college.

On the spectrum between pristine and pigpen, a godly approach to housework rests somewhere in the center. The Maid, however, parks her bootay on either end, like a teeter-totter. In one seat, she is consumed by spotless standards. In the other, she neglects her home. I've sat in both places, and I can tell you from experience that too much weight on one side will land a gal's bottom in the dirt.

Let's examine these two extremes so you can identify your tendencies toward either end. Through the filter of God's Word, we'll see how both approaches—immaculate and negligent—are unhealthy responses to the pressure women feel, whether real or perceived, to maintain a perfect household. Are you ready, ladies? It's time to fire the Maid.

## WHAT NEAT FREAKS CAN LEARN FROM JESUS

It sparkled. It gleamed. I stood over it, mop in hand, gazing at my own spectacular reflection. Yes, ma'am, that floor was *clean*. And I adored it. For about ten seconds.

Splat! A glob of mandarin oranges landed at my feet.

"Aw, come on!" I roared. "Mommy just scrubbed the floor!" My younger daughter, a baby at the time, flashed a taunting half smile from her high chair where I'd buckled her a safe distance from my mopping path. This was her revenge.

"Uh-oh!" She raised her eyebrows, as if it had been an accident—yeah, right. Just then, her older sister zoomed through the kitchen on a Tigger riding train, chugging straight through those oranges. Plastic wheels dragged a streak of citrus juice across my floor.

*Yep*, I thought. *This is my life.*

I'm wired for neatness. I like a clean house, fresh clothes, and daily shampooed hair. I brush my teeth after every meal and wash my hands incessantly. I'm afraid of germs, mud, sticky fingers, and dog licks.

Even as a teenager, I vacuumed my room every Saturday and cried when my sisters deliberately ground their sock prints into my carpet fibers immediately afterward. Siblings can be so cruel.

A healthy bent toward tidiness isn't bad. It's a responsible, grown-up trait. The problem is, tidy is tough to maintain with kids. As soon as I pick up one stack of toys, my children haul out another to spread across the room. While I wipe pudding off someone's cheeks, she grabs the spoon and smears it on my pants. Clothes stain, food spills, piles accumulate, and daughters get Elmer's glue in their ponytails. In my house, messy is a perpetual state no matter how I attempt to correct it.

But therein lies the problem. What am I *correcting*, exactly? Correction implies there's something wrong in the first place. And there is—with me, the Maid. Some days I spend more time cleaning up after my family than I do *enjoying* my family. You, too?

That is not how Jesus lived.

Jesus got dirty. He traveled dusty roads. He healed lepers. He washed grown men's feet. He pressed His lips to communal drinking cups. He was not afraid to touch disease, to hold grubby children in His arms, or to be swarmed by hordes of human beings in an era before antiperspirant, indoor plumbing, or microfiber kitchen cloths.

In order to reach people's hearts, Jesus got up close and personal with their grime.

Are we willing to do that, moms? When your child snuggles her cookie-crumb face into your shoulder, do you relish the affection or worry about chocolate smudges on your shirt? If the kids beg you to make mud pies or play paint ball, do you jump in and share their laughter or stand ready with a hose to spray them down?

*"The Word became flesh and made his dwelling among us. We have seen his glory, the glory of the one and only Son, who came from the Father, full of grace and truth" (John 1:14).*

*The Word became flesh.* Doesn't that just boggle your mind? Jesus is God. Holy, immaculate, glorious God of the universe! God didn't *have* to humble Himself in human form, descending to Earth to live among filthy, sick, unkempt people. All those fishing boats and upper rooms—seriously, they could not have smelled very good.

But He came willingly. He lived a perfect life in an imperfect, germ-infested, post-Eden environment. He made His dwelling among us in order to save us from ourselves, from our misconceptions and our faults—including my irritating compulsion to triple scrub the counter after my husband preps raw chicken. Seriously. I know I am not the only woman who does that.

I want to invest in souls more than soap. Don't you? The first step is to remember God loves us whether our floors are shiny or not. And the second step? It's to find Him in the mess.

## WHAT THAT MESS REALLY MEANS

It happens every year. Following a school break, whether Christmas or Easter or summer vacation, my house takes a hit. I'm talking total disaster. It's like Toys"R"Us blows up in my living room and I'm left to tiptoe through the shrapnel.

Last Christmas, as soon as all the presents were unleashed from their packaging, my girls scattered game pieces, stuffed animals, sticker books, lip gloss tubes, plastic tea set utensils, and Disney princess figurines across carpets and tables and sofa cushions. For an entire week I made valiant attempts to organize throughout the day, but that's the tricky thing about being on vacation—we were all home and sharing the same space and making more messes every hour. I could not keep up with my daughters' enthusiasm for playtime.

"Girls, can we please put away some of these toys?" I stood in the center of the kitchen and resisted the urge to weep.

"Sure, Momma!" Giggling trickled from their bedroom down the hall. I followed the sound and found them kneeling on the floor together, rocking their new twin dolls in their arms.

"Shhhh!" My younger one warned. "Babies are sleeping!"

"Oh, so sorry to disturb you." I backed out of their doorway, smiling.

Suddenly that mess didn't look so messy anymore.

"*Do you have eyes but fail to see, and ears but fail to hear? And don't you remember?*" (Mark 8:18).

The difference between a burden and a blessing is *perspective*. It's a matter of training our eyes to detect joy in messy places.

Are you seeing the piles of Matchbox cars or the child who loves to race them?

Are you complaining about the ice-cream drips on the counter, or will you scoop an extra bowl for yourself and join the party?

Are you mad that someone "tried on" your makeup and painted the sink with your mascara wand? Or will you bend down to kiss the face that was made in God's image, with your chin and Daddy's eyes that look up to you each morning as if you are the most beautiful woman in the world?

I'll tell you what that mess really means. *It means God gave you your kids today.* That's a gift, not a given. Yes, sometimes they're loud and needy and they can't seem to figure out how to put their socks in the hamper or their crayons back in the box. They bicker and spill and track wet boot prints in the house.

But I remind myself—*they are here with me.* They are healthy and happy and delightful. They hug my legs and tell me they love me. They beg me to make cake pops and color dinosaur pictures as if nothing else in all the world matters more than sharing ordinary moments together.

And they're right.

It's outrageous how much I love them.

And let's be honest, we all know there will come a day when our children are no longer so interested in toys or games or art projects, when their pleas to "play Monopoly with me!" or "let's build a fort!" will be fewer and farther between until they've silenced altogether. Then maybe we'll wish for one more day of dirty feet and paper scraps and Cocoa Puffs stuck in the rug.

So that disaster in my living room? I decided to celebrate it. Messes, as much as they drive me nuts, are essentially a sign that my home is filled with family, and I get to spend my days cluttering the house with my favorite people.

Of course, sometimes we need to limit the mess before everyone gets evicted. But what I'm encouraging here is balance. As moms, is it more important to keep our environment untarnished or to give our children space to learn and play and grow? I don't want my kids to grow up with memories of Mom running behind them with a hand vac. This house is their home, too.

So will you give it a try? Make some sloppy cookies, concoct a baking soda volcano, or let the kids mix sand in the kiddie pool, for goodness' sake. You're not really making a mess, tidy mom. You're making a memory.

## TO THE HOUSEWORK AVERSE: IT'S OKAY TO SCRUB THE SINK

On the opposite end of the spectrum from moms with neat-freak tendencies are the women who quit. They reach a point where it seems the house is beyond control and they can't keep up—at least not without neglecting their children, or so they fear. Therefore, they stop trying.

I've been there. And I learned something pivotal. A mother's primary job is not to entertain but to raise disciples.

"Mommy, will you play this with me?" My little one, age two at the time, peered over a mountain of heaping laundry baskets. She clutched an UNO Moo barn in her hand.

*Ugh.* I looked at her, then at the laundry, then back to my daughter again. I thought of the phrases I'd read countless times in e-mail forwards and Facebook memes. You've heard them, too, I'll bet—those modern admonishments meant to encourage weary moms.

*Days are long but the years fly by.*

*Rock and don't sweep, because babies don't keep.*

*A messy house is a happy house.*

So true! I believe that!

But then I stared down a pile of grubby socks and realized—enough, already. Seriously. This family is one day short of recycling our dirty underwear. Sometimes the laundry just has to get done.

I swallowed hard and gazed straight into my daughter's pleading eyes. "I'm sorry, sweetheart, but I cannot play right now. Mom has to do some chores."

Suddenly a strange sense of empowerment tingled through my veins. It felt a little like rebellion. Yes! I must do the chores! And that does *not* make me a bad mom!

Quite the opposite, I think.

*"She sets about her work vigorously; her arms are strong for her tasks"* (Proverbs 31:17).

While loosening ultra-tight housekeeping standards is wise, we also need to be careful not to take this approach too far. In today's child-centric culture, we moms are encouraged *so much* to spend every waking moment relishing fleeting childhood that it seems any time spent otherwise is deemed a waste, or selfish. Perhaps we don't guilt each other about our dirty floors anymore, and that's great. But now, instead, are we sheepish about *cleaning* them?

I'm taking a stand for mothers everywhere.

*It's okay to clean.*

Or to cook. Or to spend a morning running errands, paying bills, making phone calls, and folding towels. That's what grown-ups do. And how else will our kids learn unless we demonstrate?

Jesus did it first. He invited His disciples to follow Him and learn from Him *while He worked*. While He taught, healed, and prayed. As moms, our core duties are much the same. Teach. Nurture. Pray like crazy.

Back in the laundry room, I set my daughter's game on a table and clapped her hands in mine. "Sweetie, I have a great idea. You can help me put these clothes in the wash. Doesn't that sound fun?"

"Okay, Momma!" Her face lit up. "Can I push the buttons, too?"

"Absolutely. You are a good button pusher."

"Yay!" She squealed with delight as if I'd just asked her to play, well, UNO Moo or something.

Amazing, isn't it? Kids know a secret that we moms would do well to discover. *Work is play.*

## WORK YOURSELF OUT OF A JOB

Did you know your children might be capable of more than the Maid allows? One of the reasons she's so darn tired is because she takes on too much responsibility. Fortunately, as young people grow in wisdom and strength, we moms can downsize the Maid by training our kiddos to take over her tasks.

I first experienced this revelation one snowy afternoon when my daughters were ages six and three. We all pulled on snow pants and boots and stomped out the front door so I could shovel the driveway. I expected my girls to flop in the yard and make snow angels while I worked, but instead they each grabbed a shovel. So I humored them. I rattled off some instructions on how to push snow, then threw my own weight into the chore. After a few minutes I turned around and discovered my six-year-old had cleared a third of the driveway. Even her little sister helped toss a few yards of snow off the porch. Glory hallelujah, those kids cut my shoveling time in half!

When your children ask to help, do you resist? Yes, they might mess up or move slower than you. But try looking at their "help" as an opportunity to train them to take over the task. Once I figured this out, it changed my approach to housework. My younger daughter has now been folding towels since she was three. My elder daughter mixes pancake batter, scrubs the toilet, and bakes muffins from scratch. Both girls insist they can sweep the floor better than I can, and do you think I'm going to argue? Heck no. Because while my kids are juggling the broom and dustpan, I'm moving on to some other household duty and enjoying the productivity our teamwork affords.

Is that lazy, unreasonable, or cruel?

Not at all.

It's the greater purpose of parenting—*raising disciples*.

*"When Jesus had called the Twelve together, he gave them power and authority to drive out all demons and to cure diseases, and he sent them out to preach the kingdom of God and to heal the sick" (Luke 9:1–2).*

As Jesus trained His disciples to share in the work God sent Him to do, his ministry expanded. I find it interesting that He chose flawed and ordinary people to perform miracles and preach the good news. I mean, Jesus was God. He was perfectly capable of doing it all Himself—and doing it better.

Yet Jesus was not a micromanager. He empowered the people beneath Him to *be like Him*, for the benefit of generations to come.

Do you see the parallel? In a child's eyes, Mom is all-powerful, too. She's the lady who knows how to cook and clean and spell and drive. They admire you. They want to *be like you*.

So do what Jesus did. Show them how to carry out the work God designed for your family. Then your children will be enriched, your legacy will grow, and—bonus!—you'll accomplish more in less time.

## YOU ARE THE QUEEN OF YOUR CASTLE

My husband and I bought our house before we had kids, so at first our home was our baby. We lovingly stripped wallpaper and painted ceilings, refinished floors and installed new appliances. Then we scrubbed and vacuumed the place corner to corner every weekend.

A few years later, I held a toilet brush in one arm and a newborn in the other. Picture my toddler capsizing a laundry basket filled with burp rags and Dora pajamas, jumping in the pile, then spilling milk on the carpet just minutes after I'd scrubbed the stain from the day before.

With children at home, whether they're babies or toddlers or teens, housecleaning is like trying to rake the lawn in a tornado. You can scratch the grass all you want, but debris is still gonna fly, sisters. So what's the solution? Wait for the storm to pass, right? In other words, clean when the kids are gone or sleeping. But what frazzled mom wants to spend a rare quiet hour *cleaning*?

I recall one notable afternoon when my girls were small. Little sister napped in her crib while big sister was at preschool.

In those odd, tranquil moments, I usually felt pressured to relax and read a book or do something that counted as "me time." But you should've seen the sticky mystery blotches on my kitchen tile—like Venus fly traps for socks and stray cereal crumbs. The urge to clean gripped me. I *had* to scrub the floor.

At first my strategy was to get the job over with as fast as possible so I could move on to something indulgent. But as I whirled the mop across the room, it occurred to me, *this IS something indulgent.* No little legs scurried around me; no sweet voices begged to play outside. I heard only the tranquil hum of the dishwasher and my own random thoughts. So I scrubbed and scoured and sashayed through that kitchen like I owned the place.

Wait a second. I *do* own this place. Isn't that fantastic? I'm not the Maid, for crying out loud! I am the *queen*.

And this house is my castle.

When was the last time you viewed your home as a prized possession rather than a chore? Years ago, as new homeowners, my husband and I cherished our space—every wall, every countertop, every square foot of carpet was something to tend gratefully and with pride. But somehow in the daily grind of child care and clutter, my castle lost its magic. It became a loud, unceasing mess to maintain, instead of what it should be—my safe haven.

I decided that day, *I want my haven back.* So I claimed a fresh perspective on housework, and I encourage you to adopt it—for your own peace of mind.

- **Dusting is tedious.** But loving my family is not, and housework is one of the ways I care for them.

- **Wiping bathrooms is gross.** But clean tap water sure is a blessing. And so are piles of dishes and bags of groceries to unload and a thousand other conveniences that millions of people in this world live without.

- **Laundry is no party.** But sorting colors with two little girls can be a rollicking good time—especially when somebody dances around wearing underwear on her head and we all burst into giggles. (Yes, I've done that.)

Housework might be more challenging with a family underfoot. But they make your house a home, your safe haven, your castle. So never forget, beautiful moms—you are the queen.

## WHO ARE YOU VACUUMING FOR?

"Great job on the siding, Bob!" We stood in our neighbor's driveway admiring his new vinyl exterior. A small crowd of friendly faces had wandered from summer yard work to enjoy an impromptu chat. That time of year, conversation often centers on home improvement jobs.

*"Hey, Joe, I saw you put up a new play set. How do the kids like it?"*

*"How big is that pool you installed in your yard, Dave?"*

*"Is that lumber in the garage for your deck expansion, Chuck? How's that going?"*

I got to thinking of all the projects my husband does around the house—noticeable projects. The finished basement, the freshly stained fence. Brick landscape edging and a well-kept lawn.

"My husband repaved the driveway, and all the neighbors commented on how nice it looked," a friend once told me. "How come nobody congratulates me for folding laundry?"

Hmmm. Amen, sister. Why *doesn't* a woman's work get the same kudos as her man's?

Now, I realize some of you ladies sweat over glorious flower beds or climb the roof to hammer shingles yourselves. Bravo if you do. But for many of us moms, our usual household contributions are a little more obscure.

Nobody notices when I sweep the floor.

Nobody applauds when I mix oatmeal for breakfast.

Nobody drives by our house to admire my sidewalk chalk drawings or the rebate forms I stuck in the mailbox.

Just once, I want my kids to say, "Mom! You did a fantastic job grilling this cheese sandwich! You are one seriously talented woman."

But why?

Why do I need praise? Does it give my labor greater significance? Does it prove I'm a good mom?

Well, let's consider this picture in Matthew.

*Jesus traveled throughout the region of Galilee, teaching in the synagogues and announcing the Good News about the Kingdom. And he healed every kind of disease and illness. News about him spread as far as Syria, and people soon began bringing to him all who were sick. And whatever their sickness or disease, or if they were demon possessed or epileptic or paralyzed—he healed them all. Large crowds followed him wherever he went—people from Galilee, the Ten Towns, Jerusalem, from all over Judea, and from east of the Jordan River. (Matthew 4:23–25 NLT)*

Wow. Talk about a hot topic in the neighborhood. Jesus displayed supernatural healing powers and drew swarms of followers everywhere He went. If anybody had the right to boast, Jesus surely did. But do you know what comes immediately after this passage?

## THE BEATITUDES

*"One day as he saw the crowds gathering, Jesus went up on the mountainside and sat down. His disciples gathered around him, and he began to teach them. . . . 'God blesses those who are humble, for they will inherit the whole earth'" (Matthew 5:1–2, 5 NLT).*

Really? Jesus just performed a spectacle of public miracles, and then He delivered a lesson on—acclaim? Power? Validation? Nope.

*Humility.*

What does that say about how we should approach our work?

*"Whatever you do, work at it with all your heart, as working for the Lord, not for human masters, since you know that you will receive an inheritance from the Lord as a reward. It is the Lord Christ you are serving" (Colossians 3:23–24).*

Praise from people doesn't make our work more important. Knowing who we're working *for* does. And God doesn't just pat us on the back—He promises a reward! An inheritance! Can a friendly neighbor's compliments come anywhere near as cool as that?

So let those men have their repaved driveways and their shiny green lawns. The Lord sees our laundry. He sees our grocery shopping and our scrubbed bathroom floors. Next time you flip that grilled cheese, ladies, tune your ears to imagine this— the Lord of the universe is cheering you on.

*My child! You did a fantastic job! Thank you for serving Me today by taking care of your family. You are one seriously talented woman. I know—because I made you that way.*


## FIND THE CENTER OF YOUR TEETER-TOTTER

Now let's flash back to my Sunday evening snit from the start of this chapter. You'll recall the Maid was about to unleash fury on my husband. Well, she snatched that last laundry basket and huffed toward the basement stairs, through the kitchen, past the refrigerator—where a wrinkled sheet of printer paper was tacked above the ice dispenser. On it, these words were highlighted:

> *Love must be sincere. Hate what is evil; cling to what is good. Be devoted to one another in love. Honor one another above yourselves. Never be lacking in zeal, but keep your spiritual fervor, serving the Lord. Be joyful in hope, patient in affliction, faithful in prayer. Share with the Lord's people who are in need. Practice hospitality. (Romans 12:9–13)*

In my Bible, the heading of this passage is "Love in Action." And who do I love best? My family.

Ouch.

I realized at that moment that I'd been looking at my husband all wrong. I'm not his maid. I'm the *love of his life*. And love shows itself through action. Through serving and sacrifice. Through dishes and sweeping and cooking and laundry.

Do you see your housework that way? Maybe it's not a chore so much as an expression of affection for the people we serve. And if that's the case, no mound of laundry could possibly be tall enough to demonstrate my love for the man who sits on the couch while I fold his drawers.

The Maid wants to suck you into her pity party, ladies. Don't go. If I had only looked beyond myself that Sunday, I would have noticed my husband mowed the lawn. He washed the car. He grilled the chicken and fixed a clog in the sink. Between ball games on TV, he did his fair share of household work. And then he took the rest he was entitled to.

That's the center of the spectrum where God resides. Sometimes we work, sometimes we play. And sometimes we simply rest. So if you show up at my house next Sunday and my children are digging into a bag of Cheetos while I kick my feet up on the couch, don't judge. Grab a soda from the fridge and help me fold these socks. Your kids can help my kids make another mess, ensuring our cycle of "love in action" persists. Praise the Lord.

*Chapter 7*

# ATTACK OF THE ZOMBIE MOMMY

*Well, honey, you know there's a reason the Chinese used*
*sleep deprivation as a method of military torture.*
MY MOTHER, C. 2007

**Dirty Villain No. 6:** Zombie Mommy
**Evil Power:** Exhaustion
**Kryptonite:** Isaiah 40:28–31; Hebrews 4:12; Hebrews 4:16;
2 Corinthians 1:8–10; Ephesians 3:20–21; Romans 12:1;
Romans 8:16–17; Galatians 6:9; Matthew 11:28–29

---

When I was pregnant with my first daughter, one of my earliest congratulations cards came from a coworker with two children of her own. The front of the card showed a clock with the long hand at 12 and the short hand at 3. Inside she wrote, "Get used to seeing this time. That's a.m., not p.m."

Of course we chuckled, she from experience and I from pure ignorance. At that time, the thrill of pregnancy reduced impending sleeplessness to nothing more than a vague, passing thought. *Yeah, yeah, yeah,* I told myself. *I know I'll be up all night with a baby; but hey, we just got cable, so at least I'll have something to keep me occupied.*

Oh, silly girl.

Until a new mom actually experiences true sleep deprivation, she cannot possibly comprehend the suffering. It is not a joke. This is real, unrelenting pain.

## WHAT IS SLEEP DEPRIVATION?

A study published by the National Institutes of Health found that new moms get an average of 7.2 hours of sleep daily. Not so bad, right? The trouble is that their sleep is fragmented, meaning an hour here and an hour there. And let's not forget all us poor chicks whose sleep totals fall *below* average. In the newborn stage, some moms like me barely scrape together three or four hours of zzzs in a twenty-four-hour period. When babies eat and cry around the clock, Mommy's sleep cycles get interrupted for weeks and months on end. This can lead to a variety of physical and mental health issues, including mood swings, problems concentrating, and even postpartum depression.[1]

Of course, we moms don't need a scientific report to tell us that. But it is good to know we're not alone or crazy—just inhumanely tired.

I call this special symptom of motherhood "the fog." It's that state of half-dead existence in which our thoughts, actions, and emotions turn murky and dense. And who else comes slogging out of the mist but our next dirty villain, Zombie Mommy. You might recognize her. She's close cousins with the Grouch on the Couch and a distant relation to the Calendar Queen. Sadly, though, in most cases Zombie Mommy shows up through no fault of our own. She possesses our bodies for a season simply because we are parents. And children are exhausting.

## HOW LONG, O LORD?

At one point during my first pregnancy, my older sister mentioned that her babies slept through the night at six weeks old. I filed this in my mind as the textbook standard. So after my daughter was born, I reached the six-week point in eager expectation only to be woken three times a night yet again.

"I thought she'd be giving me at least a five-hour stretch by now," I complained to my parents one day. "Robin said her kids were sleeping through the night by six weeks old."

"Ha!" my dad scoffed. "Six *months* is more like it."

"*What? Six months?*"

For some of you, it was six *years*—or more.

I feel your pain. Deeply. There is no cure for sleep deprivation caused by motherhood. But there is a treatment.

> *Do you not know? Have you not heard? The* LORD *is the everlasting God, the Creator of the ends of the earth. He will not grow tired or weary, and his understanding no one can fathom. **He gives strength to the weary and increases the power of the weak.** Even youths grow tired and weary, and young men stumble and fall; **but those who hope in the** LORD **will renew their strength.** They will soar on wings like eagles; **they will run and not grow weary, they will walk and not be faint.** (Isaiah 40:28–31, emphasis added)*

## THE BIBLE IS BETTER THAN COFFEE

When my friend Alicia's fourth child was born—a characteristically horrible sleeper with reflux issues (can I get a sympathetic groan from the reflux moms?)—she sat up rocking him one evening and considered how long she'd been stuck in this nighttime routine. None of her children had slept through the night before the next baby was born. She did the mental math and realized—eight years. It had been *eight years* since she'd had a full night's sleep.

The next day, Alicia asked her husband, a family physician, "Can a woman die from sleep deprivation?"

He thought for a moment then replied, "No, sleep deprivation itself won't kill a woman. Generally it just drives her to insanity until she takes her own life."

*And we think doctors' wives have it easy.*

Alicia, like so many of us, had simply reached the threshold of her ability to cope. So she did what any faith-filled woman would do in the throes of suffering. She made a deal with God.

"I came across Hebrews 4:12 in the Amplified version of the Bible," she recalled, "which says, '*For the Word that God speaks is alive and full of power [making it active, operative, energizing and effective].*' Suddenly it was right there in front of me. God's Word is supposed to be *energizing!*"

Armed with this truth from scripture, she prayed, "Lord, I believe You can keep me alive on Your Word. I expect you to energize me, and in return I will commit that every night when I'm up with this baby, I will be in Your Word."

She bought a Bible on CD, and for months of nighttime feedings that lasted through a fifth beloved child, Alicia kept her end of the deal. Bleary-eyed and mushy brained, she listened to God's Word, night after night—and the Lord never broke His promise. Each morning, He equipped her with enough energy for the day ahead.

"In the foggiest time of my life, God brought a new clarity to me," she said. "He keeps His promises."

## PRAY FOR SUPERNATURAL ENERGY

Although my own sleepless suffering didn't last as long as Alicia's, I can certainly relate to her struggle—*and* her success. On those days when my aching body stumbled out of bed, drugged and staggering with exhaustion—when I stared down a twelve-hour stretch with no nap, no break, no brain left in my zombie head, I prayed:

*Lord, please give me a supernatural degree of energy to get through this day.*

And He did. Every time.

Does that sound too simple? Too church-lady spiritual? I hear you. Give me some *real* solutions, woman—not all this prayer and Bible stuff, right?

That's what Zombie Mommy wants you to think. Darn, that's all she's *capable* of thinking most days. She puts the milk in the pantry and the scissors in the freezer. The woman has near zero mental capacity. But *you*, Jesus-loving mom, are still in there somewhere. And you have every right to call out to God.

*"Let us then approach God's throne of grace with confidence, so that we may receive mercy and find grace to help us in our time of need" (Hebrews 4:16).*

## GOD CAN USE A GLO WORM

Even when it seems like God is distant or unaware, He is in fact intimately involved in our pain. To illustrate this truth, I'd like you to meet my friend Joy.

Joy's second child was born prematurely, which led to special feeding challenges during his first few months of life. He could ingest only small amounts of food at one time, so doctors advised Joy to feed her baby every twenty minutes around the clock.

As you can imagine, this process transformed my strong and confident friend into a shriveled version of her normal self. Even as her son began sleeping longer stretches, he still required regular nighttime feedings. So Joy endured day after day of little to no rest until her son's first birthday, when he finally started sleeping through the night.

Now after a year of sleep deprivation, Joy was desperate to function like a live person again. But God had other plans.

Doctors soon diagnosed her son with an issue requiring abdominal surgery. Talk about mommy angst; no mother enjoys sending her child into an operating room. So the day before the procedure, Joy and her family burned off some stress at the local children's museum. Somehow during the outing, her husband injured his hand but didn't tell anyone because, understandably, he didn't want to add to his wife's anxiety.

The next day, their son was admitted to the hospital, and the surgery went as planned. When the doctor called the parents to the recovery room, though, complications developed. First, their son began crying and thrashing, and they realized he was not actually awake but suffering a sleep terror. No one could rouse him.

"The doctor told me this could be a problem," Joy recalled. "And then he looked at my husband's hand and said—that's a problem, too."

Turned out Joy's husband had broken his hand and dislocated several nerves and connective tissues. He was scheduled for surgery the following day. At the same time, doctors told Joy to keep a close watch on her son because his night terrors might continue.

And continue they did—with a vengeance.

"He woke up every single night screaming his head off. You couldn't wake him up, so he would just scream and thrash at the top of his lungs—for *two hours*," Joy said.

Meanwhile, her husband's surgery left him with pins protruding from his hand, so not only was he unable to pick up the baby, but he also couldn't drive or even dress himself. Suddenly Joy was playing nurse to both her husband and her son.

Think that's enough trouble for one mom? It gets worse. Three days into this wearying routine, Joy noticed a rash on the baby's bottom, which after a warm bath quickly spread throughout half his body. Doctors suspected MRSA—a dangerous staph infection, resistant to antibiotics.

With pins in his hand, Joy's husband could not risk exposure to MRSA. On doctor's orders, he left the house, and Joy took over solo duty of caring for a sick child covered ears to toes in infection. "I had to bleach toys and blankets," she said, "and there was no rest. Every time my son went down for a nap, he'd wake up screaming."

After a week, doctors confirmed the infection was not MRSA but impetigo. Joy's husband returned home only to face another hit. Their older son had sprouted signs of chicken pox *and* ringworm.

Then Joy contracted them both.

"The ringworm was on my chest, and it hurt. But when our baby screamed, the only way I could soothe him was by holding him to my chest, so I put up with the pain," she said.

By that point, Joy felt utterly alone. Her husband remained quarantined to a separate area of the house, unable to help. And although she had a wonderful church community and a caring network of friends, nobody could step foot in her home to assist or to take one of the kids off her hands because of the risk of infection. Friends started dropping groceries on her front porch without ringing the doorbell.

All the while, her son's night terrors intensified.

"They got longer and longer, and I couldn't wake him up," Joy said. Her husband had finally recovered from surgery, yet the weeks of caring for an ill and restless household on her own had created a serious deficit in her energy and mental health. "Here it was just days before Christmas, and I was completely out of touch. I realized I hadn't left my house in two and a half months. I cried all day. I was so tired."

Sitting at her kitchen table, sobbing and blindly flipping the pages of a holiday newspaper ad, Joy began to pray out loud. "Lord, give me a break here. I am going to die or lose my mind. Just give me anything, throw me a bone—whatever You can do, Lord!"

At that moment, she opened her eyes. "I remember the

paper on the table was wet because I was crying so hard. I saw this big picture of a Glo Worm toy on the ad in front of me. The Lord said to my mind, '*Let's buy that.*'"

Joy immediately called her husband and begged him to pick up a Glo Worm. God bless him, he asked no questions. He returned home from work with a Glo Worm in hand.

That night, Joy placed the new toy in her son's crib and listened for the first telltale signs of night waking—the crinkle of his mattress protector. "It would wake me up," she explained. "I could hear it, and it would prepare me for the screaming that was going to come." This time, though, when she heard the crinkle, she waited. No crying. No whimpering. And then—she heard the lullaby song of the Glo Worm. Her son fell back to sleep, and he never had another night terror again.

"All those sleepless nights—they were the most horrific physical trial I've ever been through," Joy said. "I am so strong-willed and stubborn, for me to crumble is really a feat. But you never know what kind of faith God wants you to have. If I had been in my right mind, I would never have bought the Glo Worm. I would've said that's the dumbest thing I ever heard. I believe God brought me to the end of myself so I was crazy enough to buy it. And He used the Glo Worm to bring healing."

Eight years later, Joy can laugh about her suffering—and God's unlikely solution—because of what it taught her and others around her. "Now there's no wondering how we got through that," she said. "Nobody could help. God got the credit. I don't like it when I have to go through that kind of trial, but I love it when God gets the glory. As hard as it was, I came through it with Christ. The Lord really did take care of me."

## YOU CAN'T HANDLE IT—BUT GOD CAN

Have you heard the old saying, "God won't give you more than you can handle"? Maybe you've even spoken it a time or two. . .or twenty. Surely the sentiment is encouraging.

But it's not true.

Did you know that?

According to the Bible, God *does* in fact give us more than we can handle sometimes. No human being can muster enough strength on their own to survive the toughest circumstances—not even the über-Christians, like the apostle Paul.

> *We do not want you to be uninformed, brothers and sisters, about the troubles we experienced in the province of Asia. We were under great pressure,* **far beyond our ability to endure**, *so that we despaired of life itself. Indeed, we felt we had received the sentence of death.* **But this happened that we might not rely on ourselves but on God**, *who raises the dead. He has delivered us from such a deadly peril, and he will deliver us again.* **On him we have set our hope** *that he will continue to deliver us. (2 Corinthians 1:8–10, emphasis added)*

In this passage, Paul is writing to the church in Corinth, describing the opposition he and his travel companions faced from rioting crowds in the city of Ephesus. This persecution, in Paul's own words, was "far beyond our ability to endure." In other words, he couldn't handle it. But God could. Paul confirms this when he says, "This happened that we might not rely on ourselves but on God."

Who are you relying on? God created our bodies. He knows us inside and out. When the Lord asks a mom to withstand sleep deprivation, He knows exactly how much she can bear before she breaks. And when we reach our max capacity to endure, God takes over—as only He can.

Have no doubt, God does not refrain from giving us more than we can handle. *He helps us handle what we're given.* And in so doing, we have the opportunity to grow closer to the Lord and to experience His deliverance.

*"Now to him who is able to do immeasurably more than all we ask or imagine, according to his power that is at work within us, to him be glory in the church and in Christ Jesus throughout all generations, for ever and ever! Amen"* (Ephesians 3:20–21).

## FATIGUE AS WORSHIP

There is one more vital point we need to examine about motherhood-induced exhaustion. It's not just a test of our endurance and trust. It's a gift we can give to the Lord.

Flash back with me to a typical late-night incident in the Kopitzke home.

"Mommy?"

My eyelids popped open, startled out of sound sleep. Slowly, the hazy shape of a youngster appeared at my bedside, clutching a pillow in one hand and a doll in the other. She started to cry.

"What is it, sweetheart? What's wrong?"

"My tummy hurts!"

*Oh boy. Here we go.* I whipped off my covers and slapped two bare feet to the floor. With a hand on the small of her back, I led my five-year-old first to the bathroom for a Tums, then to the family room sofa. I tucked her beneath a warm blanket and stationed a bucket on her lap, just in case. Then I camped on the floor for the next two hours while she dozed on and off.

Nurse Mom sees plenty of nighttime action.

My kids wake at midnight from coughing fits and scary dreams.

They tiptoe to my bedroom in pitch darkness to inform me they need to go potty.

They crawl out of bed in tears because they can't find a favorite stuffed animal tucked deep beneath the covers. They expect me to find it.

They talk in their sleep.

They bump their heads on the wall.

They're thirsty. So they tap my shoulder at 2:00 a.m. asking for fresh water.

Sometimes they just want to know if it's morning yet and may they please watch TV?

*No, no, you may not. Not at three o'clock in the blessed a.m. Please go back to bed. Mommy needs her sleep.*

*I'm tired.*

Very tired.

You, too?

*"Therefore, I urge you, brothers and sisters, in view of God's mercy, to offer your bodies as a living sacrifice, holy and pleasing to God—this is your true and proper worship" (Romans 12:1).*

Have you ever thought of fatigue as worship? It never crossed my mind until a friend described her approach to surviving newborn feedings. "Every time the baby woke me up to eat," she explained, "I prayed, 'Lord, this is my sacrifice to you.'"

*My sacrifice.*

Think about that for a minute. Even if you're past the baby stage, occasional sleep loss is part of the parenting deal. Toddlers wet the bed. Teens drive the car to the basketball game. Kids of all ages wake up puking or feverish. So we worry. We ache. We run to the store at midnight for orange Gatorade. And even when the kids are sleeping safe and sound and healthy, plenty of us stay up too late scouring Pinterest, typing e-mails, or dropping JPGs into photo books because there is no earlier quiet time to indulge.

Sleep for moms is a luxury.

But this tired body, these burning, bloodshot eyeballs, these maniacal tears dripping from pure exhaustion. Could it be? It's all an offering of thanks—to the One who granted us the gift of motherhood.

> *The Spirit himself testifies with our spirit that we are God's children. Now if we are children, then we are heirs—heirs of God and co-heirs with Christ, **if indeed we share in his suffering** in order that we may also share in his glory. (Romans 8:16–17, emphasis added)*

Fatigue is physical suffering. And physical suffering can be a holy thing indeed. Consider that your struggle with sleep deprivation makes you more like Christ, who suffered unimaginable torment on the cross for you and me. When we suffer in return, Jesus sees us, He sustains us with bottomless compassion, and He fathoms the deeper value of our sacrifice.

Yes, parenting can mutate a mother into Zombie Mommy some days (or years). But these seasons of exhaustion will not last forever. So let's find the higher purpose in them while we have no choice.

*"Let us not become weary in doing good, for at the proper time we will reap a harvest if we do not give up" (Galatians 6:9).*

"Sweetheart, how does your tummy feel?" I leaned over the sofa and brushed disheveled locks of hair away from my daughter's eyes. Stiff muscles in my neck rebelled against their makeshift cot on the floor.

"Better." She cracked a weak smile.

"Do you want to go back to your bed? You'd be more comfortable there."

"No, Momma. I want to sleep in *your* bed."

*Of course,* I thought. *So do I.*

I scooped her off the sofa and carried her to my room. She snuggled into the center of our king-size mattress and fell fast asleep. I listened to the gentle rhythm of her breathing, inhaled the scent of her strawberry shampoo, and watched her cheeks glow in the moonlight.

Sleep? I do miss it terribly. But what I get in return is sweeter than a thousand naps combined.

A few hours later, I woke to sunlight peeking through the window blinds—and the dull pressure of a foot shoved against my forehead. My daughter's lanky limbs sprawled perpendicular across the bed.

*Well, Lord,* I prayed, *this is my crazy life. My sacrifice to You.*

And it's worth every exhausted minute. Amen?

*"Come to me, all you who are weary and burdened, and I will give you rest. Take my yoke upon you and learn from me, for I am gentle and humble in heart, and you will find rest for your souls"* (Matthew 11:28–29).

# Chapter 8

# NOT TONIGHT, DEAR

*My lover spoke and said to me,*
*"Arise, my darling, my beautiful one, come with me."*
Song of Songs 2:10

**Dirty Villain No. 7:** Weary Wife
**Evil Power:** Neglecting her husband
**Kryptonite:** Malachi 2:15; Ephesians 5:33; Mark 10:9;
  Proverbs 19:11; 1 Corinthians 13:4–5; Proverbs 15:1;
  1 John 4:19; Genesis 1:27; 1 Corinthians 7:3–5; Proverbs 3:27

———

One week after we brought our firstborn daughter home from the hospital, I sat trapped in an overstuffed chair in the family room with a hungry bundle in my arms. Stationed all around me were the accoutrements of new motherhood—burp cloths, baby blankets, a Boppy, my trusty tube of lanolin cream, and an industrial-strength breast pump on rental from the hospital. My husband stretched on the leather sofa across from my chair, his unshaved face peeking out beneath a tangle of quilts.

These had become our command posts.

It was a Thursday evening at eight o'clock, I remember, the hour of our favorite television show. Before the baby, my husband and I treasured those Thursday nights, when we'd snuggle in front of the TV, eat popcorn, and try to guess "who done it" before the episode concluded. Now I had no energy to follow a plot or even keep my eyes open. After several days of round-the-clock parenting, I'd lost my sense of time. Eight at night might as well have been eight in the morning for all I knew.

What happened to our old routine? Our old spark? My husband and I used to be inseparable! But now this child—our tiny, precious, helpless child—seemed to be pulling us apart.

"I miss you." Tears filled my eyes as I locked gazes with my husband across the room, unable to move or even reach for his hand because of the finally sleeping infant on my lap.

"I'm right here." He smiled.

"But it's not the same."

It might never be the same. Eventually, though, it can be even *better*.

No matter how prepared you think you are for parenting, a baby can shake a marriage like nothing else. At first it's a season, a tough baptism by fire involving sleepless nights and spats over who should change the poopy diaper. But over time, as those babies grow, we moms continue investing a large chunk of our energy and focus on keeping the kiddos fed and safe and socialized. And if we're not careful, we can lose touch with the guy who was vital to starting this crazy parenting business in the first place.

Your husband.

Remember him? Maybe you used to call him "honey" or "babe," but now he's mostly known as "Dad." He's your partner, your lover, and your very best friend. Or at least, ideally, he was at one time. And he can be again.

The majority of married moms will struggle at some point with a dirty villain I call Weary Wife. She's not necessarily malicious but rather, like the name says, weary. Parenting exhausts her and consumes her, and thus her priorities get mixed up. She dedicates the largest share of her attention to her kids and leaves very little for her husband. Sadly, she may not even realize she's doing it. Regardless of intention, though, God's design for the

Christian family remains clear throughout scripture: God first, marriage second, children third. If we stray from that order, we risk creating a chasm so wide it swallows not only our marriage but also our kids.

Who wants to seal the gap? I sure do. Let's explore four main areas in which Weary Wife erodes our marriages:

- romance
- friendship
- communication
- sex (Yes, ladies, we're going there.)

## ROMANCE: DATES AREN'T JUST FOR YOU

My daughter reached for my hand, giggling, eyes wide and sparkling with mischief. "Come on, Mom, we have a surprise for you."

I followed her downstairs to the spare bedroom. A dusty VCR sat on the floor, hooked to our ancient tube television.

"Are you ready?" My husband grinned. I settled on the edge of the bed with a toddler in my lap. Big sister bounced on her heels in excitement as she knelt beside her daddy on the carpet.

Pop! The black screen sprang to life, and I heard piano keys tinkling in the background. I recognized a white satin princess and a raven-haired prince.

Our wedding video.

I thought we had lost it. Through a couple moves and a basement flood, that priceless memento got shuffled around until nobody remembered where or when we'd seen it last. In honor of our tenth anniversary, my husband and our daughter, age four at the time, rummaged through the house until they found the videotape buried in a box. This was my anniversary gift.

Tears leaked down my cheeks as I relived every frame—the white roses, the vows, the dress my mother made.

"Do you like it, Momma?"

"I love it, sweetheart. This is the best surprise ever."

Suddenly, my daughter's smile melted to trembling lips. She climbed onto the bed next to me and bawled into my shoulder.

"My goodness, what's wrong?" Her dad and I exchanged baffled looks. "Did something upset you? Why are you sad?"

"No, Mom, I'm not sad," she choked. "I'm crying because I'm happy!"

That's when I realized—I need to keep dating my husband.

Date night was not always our greatest strength. At the time of the wedding video discovery, it had been seven months since our last dinner outing without kids. Excuses come easy when we're busy raising small children. We're tired, babysitters cost more than the restaurant bill, my babies want me to tuck them in—they'll miss me. They *need* me.

Except, no they don't. Not on date night. Not as much as they need two parents united, strong, and in love.

*"Has not the one God made you? You belong to him in body and spirit. And what does the one God seek? Godly offspring. So be on your guard, and do not be unfaithful to the wife of your youth"* (Malachi 2:15).

As parents, we have a responsibility to raise godly children— to give them every advantage in their journey toward claiming Jesus as their own. This begins with living by example. One important way we can show our kids how much we love and want to obey the Lord is by nurturing a Christ-centered marriage. God's Word tells us, *"Each one of you must love his wife as he loves himself, and the wife must respect her husband" (Ephesians 5:33).* Are we going to mess up sometimes? Sure. All couples go through rough seasons, discontentment, and occasional arguments. No marriage is perfect. Yet even our mistakes and misgivings afford us opportunities to demonstrate our faith in action—through humility and forgiveness.

So what does that mean for my family and yours? Well, I learned the hard way. A strong relationship requires spending quality time together. My children need to see Mom fluttery with anticipation of a night alone with Dad. They need to watch Dad clasp Mom's fingers while he leads her out the door, blowing kisses to two little girls already immersed in the babysitter's nail polish collection.

They need to know Mom and Dad are here for them because we're here for each other first.

How are you doing in this area?

It's risky to convince ourselves we're fine without regular dates—without time set aside to nurture our relationship, to rekindle the fire, to remember *why we chose this person*, and *why we love being with this person* more than anybody else in the world. Because we can get so absorbed in the routines and responsibilities—the teaching, cooking, cleaning, running, child-centric activities of each day—that we forget to make eye contact when we talk to one another. Then we forget to ask, *What's on your mind?* Or, *What are your dreams?* Until one day we wake up pondering dangerous questions like, *Who are you?* and *What happened to the person I once pursued with all my heart?*

Nobody sets out *intending* to drift, do they? So how does it happen? Dates can't hurt. They can only help.

"*Therefore what God has joined together, let no one separate*" *(Mark 10:9).*

Maybe you can't afford dinner out, and that's okay. Share a frozen pizza after the kids go to bed. Eat it on a picnic blanket with candles or go sit on the back porch with a baby monitor plugged in. Trade child care with another trusted family. Meet in the kitchen for lunch when the kids are at school. There are hundreds of ways to enjoy an affordable date with your spouse. The point is to drop the excuses and make it happen.

Why? Because when I witnessed our daughter's sweet, un-filtered reaction to a video of her parents giddy in love, I caught a glimpse of my marriage through her eyes. And I finally under-stood. Date night isn't just for a husband and wife. Our children need it as much as we do.

## FRIENDSHIP: YOUR HUSBAND IS NOT YOUR ENEMY

At the core of married love is a mutual *like* for each other. Maybe you haven't dug it up in a while, but chances are a fundamental affinity for your spouse still dwells somewhere in your heart—and his.

Weary Wife tends to forget this detail.

I know firsthand.

It was a plastic ball, okay? A silly thing, really. Hanging from five feet of twine tied to the rafters, this shiny red weapon glared at me as I pulled our minivan into the garage. I stared back, sur-prised, and my eyes narrowed. The blood in my veins pumped harder.

*A ball, eh? Who does he think he is, hanging a ball from the ceiling as if I don't know how to park my own van in my own garage? There is nothing wrong with the way I park. If he thinks I creep a little too close to his recycling bins and his precious lawn mower, well, that's not my problem. But this! This ball makes his problem my problem.*

Weary Wife was livid.

"I take offense to that ball in the garage." I hung my keys and faced my husband in a standoff.

"Why?" He crinkled his eyebrows.

"Because it implies I'm too stupid to know how to park the van. I know how to park the van."

"I just thought it would be helpful, that's all."

"No, you thought you would teach me a lesson in parking. I don't need it, thankyouverymuch."

"It's just a ball. I didn't mean anything by it."

He peeked through the kitchen entry window into the garage and saw what I thought of his little ball. I'd pulled the van a good two feet past it—on purpose—and the twine hung at a 45-degree angle across my windshield. *Take* that, *Jack*.

And yet. My husband seemed genuinely confused by my reaction. Hurt, even. In fact, I think he expected me to *thank* him for his handy ball trick.

Funny, isn't it, how two people can look upon the same scene and see entirely different pictures. My husband saw *helpful*. I immediately saw *insulting*.

Guess which one of us needed a vision checkup.

*"A person's wisdom yields patience; it is to one's glory to overlook an offense"* *(Proverbs 19:11).*

Are you easily offended? Do you default to anger before considering the other side of the story? I confess this had become a habit for me in marriage. I often assumed my husband was trying to irk me when he really meant no harm.

If you can relate to that, I encourage you to ask yourself three very important questions.

## 1. Is my husband my friend or my enemy?

In relationships, we have a choice, and it goes much deeper than deciding whether or not to be irritated. We must first choose to believe our husbands have good intentions. It's basic, but as wives I think we lose sight of this far too often.

My husband is my friend. He doesn't wake up every morning plotting his next attack. We're on the same team. He loves me and wants the best for me. So why should I automatically assume his goal is to annoy me? Even if his words and actions don't come out right, they are not darts aimed at my heart. Retaliation is the wrong answer. My husband deserves the benefit of my doubt. He deserves my love.

And what is love?

*"Love is patient, love is kind. It does not envy, it does not boast, it is not proud. It does not dishonor others, it is not self-seeking, it is not easily angered, it keeps no record of wrongs"* (1 Corinthians 13:4–5).

If you remember nothing else from this chapter, ladies, please own this: Your husband is not your enemy. He's your friend. This simple shift in perception can transform a marriage.

## 2. Is this worth ruining my day?

When I pulled into the garage that afternoon, imagine if I'd employed this thought process before opening my mouth:

- *If I bark about the ball thing, it could lead to an argument.*
- *An argument could tank the entire day.*
- *Is this worth ruining my day?*

I'm not saying we should avoid healthy conflict, but really, is conflict always necessary? Try overlooking an offense and see how it changes your heart.

## 3. What else could he have meant by that?

If you vote to go the conflict route, then it's your responsibility to get your husband's side of the story—before you snap. In my case, "Honey, why did you hang that ball in the garage?" would've been a perfectly peaceful introduction. Then maybe I could've averted anger in the first place.

Sound familiar? Think back to the lesson we gleaned from the Grouch on the Couch about "putting a little love in your voice." It applies to marriage as well as parenting.

*"A gentle answer turns away wrath, but a harsh word stirs up anger"* (Proverbs 15:1).

## THE COUPLE THAT PLAYS TOGETHER STAYS TOGETHER (PUN INTENDED)

Recently I popped a question to my friends on Facebook asking if anyone engages in recreational activities with their husbands purposely for the sake of staying friends. Their answers were inspiring. Some of them run side by side, training for half marathons. Others enjoy spending time together in the yard, tending vegetable and flower gardens. Friends told me they go fishing, biking, bowling, and cross-country skiing. One couple takes a spin class together for exercise *and* quality time.

Wives step out of their comfort zones to shoot darts with their husbands; husbands man up in dance lessons with their wives. All because they know *friendship* is a vital component of a strong marriage. And one of the best ways a husband and wife can nurture their friendship is by playing together—literally.

"It all started because we wanted to set a better New Year's resolution," my friend Sarah told me. She and her husband were already making regular date nights a priority—praise the Lord— but they were tired of the same old dinner-and-a-movie routine. "We wanted something we could actually engage in together rather than sitting at a restaurant talking about the kids, or going to a dark theater where you can't talk, anyway."

So they chose guitar lessons.

Understand—guitar was a new frontier for Sarah. She had never played before. But, determined to share an adventure, she and her husband saved for two months to buy instruments. Then they scheduled lessons together every other week for six months. When Sarah crunched the numbers, she figured their lessons cost no more than a restaurant tab and movie tickets.

"Learning guitar together opened up a whole new window of discovering new things about each other," Sarah said. "My husband would practice and sing songs to me at home, so our biweekly dates spilled over into our everyday connection." And—major bonus—their kids saw the intention behind Mom and Dad's new joint interest and were profoundly encouraged by it.

What can you do to build up your friendship with your husband? Find an activity you'll both enjoy and make plans to do it. Yes, it might be a hassle. It might even be hard. But your marriage is worth all that and more.

## COMMUNICATION: ARE YOU SPEAKING HIS LANGUAGE?

Words of affirmation. Acts of service. Receiving gifts. Quality time. Physical touch. These are the five love languages defined by bestselling author and pastor Dr. Gary Chapman.[1] The premise of the love languages phenomenon is that if you *express* love in the way that *speaks* love to your spouse, you can improve communication and strengthen your marriage.

It takes some practice to get this down.

"You are so handsome." I batted my lashes at my hubby from across the kitchen table. He kept his eyes fixed on a magazine and stuck out his tongue. "I adore you," I crooned again. "Do you know what a great dad you are?"

"Uh-huh." He looked up. "Hey, do you know how late the dry cleaner is open?"

"The dry cleaner?" My face drooped. "Didn't you hear what I said? I'm pouring my heart out to you here, and you're talking about the dry cleaner."

"What. . . I need to pick up my shirts. Would you hand me those chips, please?"

Heaven help us.

My love language? Words of affirmation. Tell me I'm special, compliment my hair or my character or my casserole. Reassure me with words that say you love me, then I will feel loved.

My husband, on the other hand, is not a gushy words guy. I

could tell him a hundred times a day what a brilliant, sexy specimen of divine workmanship he is, but it wouldn't register nearly as much as taking out the garbage, because my husband values acts of service more than words of affirmation.

Compliments don't come naturally to him, but every once in a while he surprises me. Like one Saturday morning that I will never forget.

"What are you doing, Beautiful?"

I turned around to see who he was talking to. There were only two people in the kitchen—my husband and the frumpy lady in a faded apron who was poking toothpicks into a batch of muffins. My husband looked straight at me and smiled, so clearly he was referring to the muffin frump. I smiled back.

"I'm checking to see if these muffins are done. Do you want one?"

"Sure. I love your muffins." He patted my tush and walked away. Inside, my heart squealed. *He called me beautiful! Yay!*

Fast-forward half a day. I tackled a typical weekend to-do list—laundry, e-mails, baking. But when I trekked to the basement to throw in a load of wash, I spotted our mess of hand-me-down clothing bins scattered across my husband's workshop. These were my responsibility—a project I'd been putting off because it wasn't urgent and, quite frankly, the disorganized clothes didn't bother me. I wasn't the one who had to step over the haphazard piles to reach the hammer and duct tape. That was my husband's problem.

Or was it mine?

Earlier that morning, my sweet hubby had stretched beyond his natural bent in order to speak my love language. I realized at that moment that I needed to sacrifice my own agenda to speak back—in the language he knew best. So I put aside the laundry, heaved a deep sigh, and hauled those clothing bins to the living room for some serious decluttering. Three hours later, my husband had a clear path to his workbench. And I had a better understanding of how to love him.

Think of it this way. Imagine if I gave my husband a Kitchen Aid mixer for his birthday instead of new hunting boots. Because, of course, I would swoon to see a shiny Kitchen Aid sitting on the counter. *Eeek! It's what I've always wanted!* But it's not what my husband wants. He drools over hunting boots. So it'd be pretty ridiculous to give him *my* heart's desire for *his* birthday, right? How would I feel if he gave me hunting boots for mine? Yuck.

Of course we *know* we love each other. But I *feel* loved best when my husband shows it in the way that speaks to my heart. And so does he. Isn't God funny? Often he pairs two people with opposite love languages in order to teach them how to love unconditionally.

*"We love because he first loved us" (1 John 4:19).*

So do your marriage a huge favor. Learn your husband's love language, and encourage him to learn yours. Weary Wife cannot thrive for long in a home where love is spoken loud and clear.

## S-E-X: JUST DO IT

And while we're on the subject of love. Sometimes we must do more than speak it.

We have to *make* it, too.

Oh, girls, I know you don't want to hear that. I'm female, I get it. I know all the excuses. Between you and me, I don't totally *disagree* with all the excuses. We're tired. We've had little people climbing over us all day. These boobs are a feeding trough now, not a toy! Plus a woman's libido is just lower—that's a scientific fact, okay? We don't *need* sex as much as our man does.[2]

True. But none of that changes the fact that *he still needs it.*

The stats might be startling to a woman. Research indicates

between 80 and 90 percent of men name sexual intimacy as the most important component in a marriage.[3] Even if your husband falls into the 20 percent minority, it's likely that sex is still high on his list—and quite possibly more important to him than it is to you. Sex for a man is a physical, emotional, and spiritual need. Let's examine each of these in detail.

## SEX IS A PHYSICAL NEED

*"So God created mankind in his own image, in the image of God he created them; male and female he created them" (Genesis 1:27).*

God invented our bodies. He made men and women different yet complementary. (Should we draw a picture?) And of course God is supercreative, so He wired men to build up and release sexual tension on a regular basis, while women are designed to, um, help.[4]

But what if you just don't feel like "helping"?

Think of it this way. For your husband, sex is like food. It's a physiological need. He must have it or he'll die! (Well, not exactly, although for him it probably feels that way sometimes.) How would you feel if you were starving and your husband refused to feed you? Worse than that, imagine if he actually stood in front of you dangling a delicious platter of succulent morsels—pineapple, cheesecake, pizza, chocolate!—but as soon as you reached to grab a bite, he yanked the platter away and said, *"Oh, sorry, I'm not in the mood to feed you. Maybe tomorrow."*

Some of you might be thinking, *I am not a slice of pizza, thank you very much.* I realize this is a delicate issue in a lot of marriages, and I'm not trying to make light of it. I'm only encouraging you to see sex from a husband's perspective. Could it be possible that your troubles in this area might be rooted, at least partially, in your own misunderstanding of your husband's needs?

If you have a problem with your stud's sex drive, please talk to God. Pray about this very important aspect of your marriage. Seek counseling or a doctor's care if necessary. God created your husband to want you, and that is a good thing. It's a compliment! And remember that God does not make mistakes. Therefore, there must be more to this sex business than Weary Wife can see from her side of the bed. Read on.

## SEX IS AN EMOTIONAL NEED

As women, we tend to feel closer to our husbands when we engage in meaningful conversation. So imagine if your husband went on a business trip, and after Skyping one evening, he says, "Well, honey, it's been nice catching up with you. Let's chat again when I get home in three weeks."

Three weeks!? No way! You want to hear from him at least daily, right? And that is how your husband feels about sex, ladies. When you allow the gap between intimate encounters to stretch over days and weeks and months, he loses touch with you. He *misses* you.

Now I'm not saying you must get busy every night of the week. How often you canoodle with your man is a decision the two of you should make together. Have you ever asked him? Be brave. Be vulnerable. Initiate the conversation. Sex is not meant to be a one-sided deal. Your husband wants you to enjoy him, too. Simply bringing up the subject can be a gentle first step in connecting with him emotionally.

## SEX IS A SPIRITUAL NEED

There's another good reason we should not deprive our husbands, and it has to do with way more than making him happy.

*The husband should fulfill his marital duty to his wife, and likewise the wife to her husband. The wife does not have authority over her own body but yields it to her husband. In the same way, the husband does not have authority over his own body but yields it to his wife. Do not deprive each other except perhaps by mutual consent and for a time, so that you may devote yourselves to prayer. Then come together again* **so that Satan will not tempt you** *because of your lack of self-control. (1 Corinthians 7:3–5, emphasis added)*

Did you catch that?

Married sex wards off Satan.

A key weak spot in which the enemy aims to attack marriage is physical intimacy. Problems in this area—particularly depriving or rejecting your husband regularly—can erode a man's confidence[5] and drive a serious wedge between you. It opens the door for all sorts of sin, including resentment, guilt, temptation, and pride.

On the other hand, fulfilling your mutual need for emotional and spiritual connection *through sex* can strengthen and empower a married couple against the devil's schemes. When Weary Wife neglects her husband sexually, she misses a beautiful opportunity to support his spiritual desire for purity.

"It's like pie," my friend Tammy told me. "When you're starving, that pie looks awfully good. But after you've had a few pieces, you're full." Because Tammy's husband travels regularly for work, she makes sure he gets his fill of pie at home. "That way," she explained, "when a tasty slice walks past him in an airport, he doesn't even want to look at it."

Ladies, consider that sex is the one gift only *you* can give your husband. So *"Do not withhold good from those to whom it is due, when it is in your power to act"* (Proverbs 3:27). In Focus on the Family's series Understanding Your Husband's Sexual Needs, Dr. Juli Slattery put it this way:

*Your husband depends on you to be his partner in his battle against sexual temptation. Although you aren't responsible for his actions, you are a key component in his victory. You're the only woman in the world whom your husband can look at sexually without compromising his integrity! . . . Please understand: You aren't responsible for your husband's sexual behavior. Don't be motivated out of fear that he will act out if you don't meet his needs; rather be motivated out of love and a desire to share his spiritual journey with him.*[6]

## COMMITMENT IS A CHOICE

Beyond romance, beyond friendship and sex, there is one overarching weapon we can wield against Weary Wife's offense.

The decision to stay.

When my husband's youngest brother got married, we had already celebrated eleven years of wedded bliss plus two kids and a minivan. Surely we had this marriage thing *down*.

Or so I thought. Until a moment during the ceremony when the minister spoke these words: "Marriage isn't a vow you make once and for all on your wedding day. It's a daily recommitment."

Huh. A daily recommitment—to love, honor, and cherish this person, in sickness and in health—every single stinking day, whether you feel like it or not.

I turned to look at my husband, the tallest groomsman on the altar, standing regal and proud among a line of young men. *He's still my groom,* I thought. *He's still the one I love.*

This man, whom I know beyond the tuxedo.

The one who mows the lawn in hole-torn jeans and a sweaty three-day beard.

The one who clutched my hand through childbirth and whispers bedtime stories to our girls.

The one who harbors dreams still not reached, and cheers me on toward mine.

I know his virtues. I know his faults. Do I still wake up every day vowing "I do"? When his hair peppers gray and he gains a few pounds. When we go to bed in silence the night before, angry and hurt. When other people or places start to look more interesting than this life we share. Will I lay it all on the altar again each morning and promise to love my husband most?

If there's anything I've learned since my own wedding day, it's that the exhilaration of new love fades. But it can grow to something deeper, something even stronger.

Commitment.

And commitment isn't a feeling. It's a choice.

At my brother-in-law's reception, I watched with my heart stuck in my throat as my husband spun our six-year-old daughter on the dance floor. Someday—in a blur of years like a single breath—I'll look on this same scene at our daughter in shimmering white, and her daddy blinking back tears as he gives her away to her own husband, her own lifelong choice. And I pray it'll be a good one.

Because marriage still matters. It's the love of God growing through generations in good times and bad. And I'm going to choose it again and again, day after day, till death do us part.

Will you?

# Chapter 9

# MARTYR MOM AIN'T NO GOOD GUY

*Be who God meant you to be and you will set the world on fire.*
CATHERINE OF SIENA

**Dirty Villain No. 8:** Martyr Mom
**Evil Power:** Neglecting herself
**Kryptonite:** Philippians 2:3–4; Galatians 5:14; Deuteronomy
4:9; 1 John 4:16; 1 Peter 2:9; 1 Peter 4:10; 1 Timothy 3:5;
Philippians 4:6–7; Psalm 51:6–10; 16–17; 1 Corinthians
6:19–20; James 1:2–4; 1 John 1:9; Proverbs 28:9;
2 Corinthians 7:10; Romans 8:1; Psalm 34:4–5;
2 Corinthians 10:18

---

Tell me something.

Who are you?

No, really. Who *are* you?

Before I had children, if you'd asked me that question, I would've said I'm a Christian. I'm a wife. I'm a writer, a singer, a friend. I'm an optimist! A dreamer. A big Jane Austen buff.

And you? How did you define yourself before kids?

Fast-forward to the present day. Ask me who I am, and I'll tell you straight up I'm a mom. Yes, I'm still a Christian, a wife, an optimist, and a dreamer. I still love Jane Austen novels, even if I have no time to read them. But how I view my place in the world has changed considerably since my children arrived. I'm responsible for other human beings now. They hold a huge piece of my heart and head. Parenting isn't just what I do, it's *who I am*. Right?

Well. . .not quite.

Our final dirty villain is perhaps the most dangerous of all, because she is often mistaken for a good guy. I call her Martyr Mom. Can you guess her evil power?

Martyr Mom sacrifices herself for the sake of serving her family.

Wait a second. Sacrifice is good, right? Sacrifice is godly! Ah, true—to a point. God's Word has much to say about sacrifice and selflessness, yes. The trouble comes when we isolate the concept of sacrifice and thereby misinterpret the Bible's full intent. Then we sacrifice, sacrifice, sacrifice to our own detriment, as well as our family's.

Ladies, we're about to pull the mask from Martyr Mom's ugly face. She is your persecutor, not your friend.

## THE BATTLE AGAINST UNHEALTHY SELFLESSNESS

I know Martyr Mom's schemes. I know them very well. Of all the dirty villains we've faced so far, Martyr Mom was once my closest ally—or so I thought. In fact, I believed God was telling me to join forces with her for my own good. I heard His command in verses like these:

> *Do nothing from selfish ambition or conceit, but in humility count others more significant than yourselves. Let each of you look not only to his own interests, but also to the interests of others. (Philippians 2:3–4 ESV)*

> *For the entire law is fulfilled in keeping this one command: "Love your neighbor as yourself." (Galatians 5:14)*

I zeroed in on the "do nothing from selfish ambition" and "count others more significant than yourselves" parts. Surely that meant suppressing my own needs and wants, right? Think of *others*, not yourself! Give, give, give! Ask for nothing in return.

In recent years, however, God has taken me on a journey to examine these scriptures more accurately, in light of His gentle grace. And it makes all the difference.

*"Let each of you look not only to his own interests. . ."*

Note this verse does not say, "*Do not* look to your own interests." Rather, it says, "look *not only* to [your] own." In other words, consider other people's interests *in addition to* your own. Which must mean *it's okay to consider your own interests.* And—are you ready for this?—it might actually be a sin *not to*.

Because "Love your neighbor as yourself" does not say, "Love your neighbor *instead of* yourself," or even "Love your neighbor *more than* yourself." No, God really wants us to love other people, so He says to "love your neighbor *as yourself*."

Do you see? *The Bible assumes we love ourselves—a lot.*

And what does it mean to love yourself? We're not talking about vanity, pride, or shallow self-esteem. The Hebrew root word for "love" in this instance is *aheb*, which is the type of love people feel for each other and for God. It's a deep heart-to-heart connection, admiration, familiarity, enjoyment, and trust—in other words, the healthy kind of love. That is what God wants us to have for ourselves. After all, He created you. He thinks you're pretty special.

Do you?

*"Only give heed to yourself and keep your soul diligently, so that you do not forget the things which your eyes have seen and they do not depart from your heart all the days of your life; but make them known to your sons and your grandsons."*
*(Deuteronomy 4:9 NASB)*

Give heed to yourself, sweet mommas. *Keep your soul diligently.* When we tend to our own souls and love the person God created in us, we will be more fully able to recognize and appreciate "the things which our eyes have seen"—our blessings, God's promises and His faithfulness. Then He tells us, *don't let them depart from your heart.* Hold them close all the days of your life. *Pass them on to your children.*

Wow. Think about that. Loving yourself and your Creator enough to take care of your soul (His masterpiece!) will better enable you to teach and guide your children. So, ironically, taking care of yourself is in effect one of the best ways you can *give, give, give* to your family. Martyr Mom has it all backward.

When we're maxed out on motherhood, when we're exhausted, grouchy, envious, worried, overworked, and discontent because we haven't considered our own emotions or needs for days or weeks, what happens to our poor souls? We allow the dirty villains to beat them down, to pummel the very core of our being. We lose sight of "the things which our eyes have seen." We miss out on opportunities to share God with our children.

Shouldn't we love ourselves enough to fight back?

*"And so we know and rely on the love God has for us. God is love. Whoever lives in love lives in God, and God in them" (1 John 4:16).*

Because God is love and He dwells in us through faith, we, too, have tremendous access to share His love—with others and with ourselves. Yes, I know, as moms we spend most of our time taking care of other people. It's the nature of the job. But by taking care of ourselves, too, we give our families a happier, stronger, more complete version of us—and we teach our kids how to love themselves the way God intended.

Let's talk about four important ways we can "keep our souls diligently."

- Expand your identity beyond motherhood.
- Release your true feelings.
- Protect the temple.
- Ditch the mom guilt.

## WHO AM I, AND WHY AM I HERE?

Motherhood can consume us, can't it? God gave us this job, and He calls us to do it well. Nurturing His children may require the majority of our time and energy, and that's okay. That's normal.

But it's not everything. As important as motherhood is, in God's plan it's still just *a* role we play—not *the* role.

*"But you are a chosen people, a royal priesthood, a holy nation, God's special possession, that you may declare the praises of him who called you out of darkness into his wonderful light" (1 Peter 2:9).*

According to scripture, our primary purpose in life is not parenting. Or marriage. Or landing a great position. What you *do* is not who you *are*. If you have faith in Christ, then your identity is first and foremost not as a mom but a *child*—God's child, His special possession. You've been *chosen*. Why?

*"That you may declare the praises of him who called you. . . ."*

You and I exist to bring glory to God. We can do that through parenting, definitely. We glorify God every time we change a diaper or pack a school lunch. Motherhood is a high and holy calling. But it might not be our *only* calling.

A few years ago, I was scheduled to sing with my church worship band for Easter. My family is part of a large congregation, and our holiday services typically involve a special production requiring extra rehearsals. At the time, my girls were ages four and one—a needy stage—and I struggled to leave them in the evenings for practice sessions. One night, as the kids clung to my legs and begged me not to go, I groaned to my husband.

"Maybe I just shouldn't sing at church anymore. It's too hard on the family."

"Honey," he replied, "sometimes you need to serve more people than just us."

Bless him. Those words changed my life.

God gave each of us particular gifts and talents, and He wants us to use them. For some women that means pursuing activities, ministry, or work we can accomplish from home or within the family routine. For others, it might mean stepping outside the family to serve God. I'm so grateful my husband recognized—at a time when I'd lost sight—that motherhood was not my only calling in life. Because of his support, I went on to lead Bible studies and serve wholeheartedly in women's ministry at our church. I chased my passion for writing. And I still sing on the worship team. Those pursuits have stretched me, blessed me, and fulfilled me in ways motherhood does not. Family is still my top priority. But by allowing room in my hectic momma life for interests beyond parenting, I can show my kids what it looks like to serve God by serving other people—without sacrificing the whole person God created me to be.

*"Each of you should use whatever gift you have received to serve others, as faithful stewards of God's grace in its various forms" (1 Peter 4:10).*

Now. This is where I need to "hit the pause button," as my pastor would say. Let me be clear. Serving your family *does* qualify as serving others. For those of you who desire to be home, to serve God by devoting your attention almost exclusively to your husband and children, I agree it is *enough* to be a wife and mom. You do not need to spread yourself thin across many activities in order to please God; in fact, we explored in chapter 5 how the Calendar Queen can distract us from our very purpose of praising God.

But for those of you, like me, who believe your desires to pursue interests beyond motherhood are inspired by God and *for* God, I encourage you to prayerfully consider each opportunity. Martyr Mom will whisper, *Don't do it.* But God can drown her out.

Here are five practical steps to follow when deciding whether or not to pursue an activity outside of the family—including work, ministry, hobbies, or goals.

## 1. Pray.

Make no decisions without consulting God and His Word. If an opportunity directly contradicts God's commands in scripture, turn away and don't look back.

## 2. If you're married, get your husband's buy-in.

Moving ahead without his support can create major problems down the road. If you're a single mom, talk with a trusted friend who can help hold you accountable or provide child care. The two of you need to agree that this pursuit will *enhance* and not harm your family. Consider the wise words of 1 Timothy 3:5, *"If anyone does not know how to manage his own family, how can he take care of God's church?"*

## 3. Set boundaries.

During a particularly busy season, I found myself focused more on my laptop than on my kids. So I made a decision not to turn on a computer unless my children were asleep or at school. That way I could clearly prevent my writing pursuits from crossing over into family time. It was tough but definitely worthwhile. I learned to live in the moment as well as become more discerning about the projects I took on.

## 4. Reevaluate regularly.

How are your activities affecting the family? How are they affecting you? Weigh the pros and cons, and invite your husband's input. Remember that the purpose of any outside pursuit is to bring glory to God. If your activities are causing consistent discord in the family, consider that they may be defeating the purpose.

## 5. Resist the temptation to compare yourself to other women.

Some of us need only a quick bubble bath to feel refreshed and fulfilled; others need a hobby, a goal, or a regular commitment beyond the family. Be careful not to judge your sisters in Christ or assume you're faulty for needing more or less time away. Focus on your personal relationship with God and His calling in *your* life, rather than analyzing the lives of other women.

## RELEASE YOUR TRUE FEELINGS

My friend Jamie moved from Texas to a large Wisconsin home that begged for a few modern updates. After spending several months and thousands of dollars gutting and replacing every inch of her kitchen, a plumbing leak destroyed the whole thing—on Christmas Eve, no less, with a house full of relatives visiting from out of state. The kitchen had to be entirely redone. In the weeks that followed, an army of deafening industrial dryers camped on Jamie's ground floor, and she was forced to stay at a hotel with her two kids. I should mention her husband traveled extensively for work, so she was left in charge of the repairs.

A group of us ladies sat around the table at our weekly Bible study listening to Jamie share an update on her remodel horror story. "I know I need to keep this all in perspective," she concluded, like an apology. "It's really not that bad."

*Not that bad.* Now if your ceiling had just crashed into your kitchen while you were slicing the Christmas ham, would you be a little stressed? Uh, yeah. But good Christian women are taught to have this "perspective" thing, which prevents us from fully acknowledging our heartache.

It comes out in phrases like this.

*But the situation could've been much worse.*

*Other people have bigger problems than mine.*

*I know I'm blessed. So I shouldn't complain.*

Yes, yes that's true. The Bible does say "do everything without grumbling" (Philippians 2:14), so you have no right to do that. But you do have a right to *speak truth*. And sometimes the truth is we feel frustrated, mad, disappointed, or hurt. God made us emotional beings, did He not? He designed us to feel.

Now I'm not saying "trust your feelings" because, as we examined in chapter 3, the heart is inherently deceitful (Jeremiah 17:9), and we're called not to indulge it but to guard it (Proverbs 4:23). But how? How do we guard something that is by nature a wild beast?

We don't.

God does.

> *Do not be anxious about anything, but in every situation, by prayer and petition, with thanksgiving, present your requests to God. And the peace of God, which transcends all understanding,* **will guard your hearts and your minds** *in Christ Jesus. (Philippians 4:6–7, emphasis added)*

When we open our heart-gates wide to the Lord, welcoming Him into every nook and cranny, He can examine, console, heal, and restore. This is not a process reserved just for the "big problems" in life. It's a daily surrender.

And it requires vulnerable conversations with the Lord.

*"Behold, you delight in truth in the inward being, and you teach me wisdom in the secret heart. . . . Create in me a clean heart, O God, and renew a right spirit within me"* (Psalm 51:6, 10 ESV).

God desires truth in the inward being, the heart. Consider

maybe He allows some trials in our lives not so we would "perspective" them away, but so we would acknowledge the truth of the hurt or frustration. So we would feel it deeply enough to bring it to Him.

What if we looked at our trials—big or small—as an *invitation* from God? He wants to hear from us. Are you going to talk?

Oh, that's right. There's nothing to talk about. Because Martyr Mom is fine, eh? She's blessed. No complaints here.

*Uh-huh.*

God deserves more than a surface relationship with us. So do our husbands, children, close friends, and sisters in Christ. If we brush authentic heartache under the rug and convince ourselves we're not really bothered because we're not "supposed" to be, we have cheated God of His divine right to fellowship with us, and we've lost an opportunity to connect on a deeper level with fellow believers.

So your new kitchen flooded? Your kids have been throwing up all week? Your stylist turned your bangs pink? Darn, girl. Do the ugly cry if you have to. God can take it. Your friends will hand you tissues. And yes, you *are* blessed, and God knows you know it. You're mighty grateful for all the things going right in your life. You should be.

Just don't let your gratitude suppress your honesty, Martyr Mom. That's not being holy. That's called *denial*—which is really a fancy word for lying.

When Jamie's kitchen was restored and the stress of it all faded to a memory, she could finally laugh about it. But not right away. In the midst of a trial, we walk that strange line between gratitude and grief. It's a lifelong tug-of-war, really. The more we learn to embrace both joy and sorrow, the closer we'll grow to the God who grants us both. And to know God, well, that is by far the greatest blessing of all.

*"You do not delight in sacrifice, or I would bring it; you do not take pleasure in burnt offerings. My sacrifice, O God, is a broken spirit; a broken and contrite heart you, God, will not despise"* (Psalm 51:16–17).

## PROTECT THE TEMPLE

Acknowledging our emotional needs is just part of the journey toward keeping our souls in shape. Our spiritual well-being is also closely tied to our physical health. As with so many other lessons in motherhood, I learned this one the hard way.

A few years ago, on what was supposed to be an ordinary Sunday morning, I found myself in the emergency room for symptoms resembling a stroke. One side of my face and my limbs went numb, my hands shook, and I felt strangely light-headed. Doctors scanned my brain and my heart but found nothing, so they sent me home.

Five months later, I landed in the hospital again, this time for intense abdominal pains—like contractions without a prize at the end. After another gamut of tests, doctors found nothing. I spent the entire next day sleeping off the morphine they'd pumped into my body. That was another Sunday.

Mother's Day.

Ultimately, all of my symptoms were attributed to stress. And I realized Martyr Mom had stolen from me the one day of the year I labeled "acceptable" for taking a break.

Do you think God was trying to tell me something?

Over time, the Lord revealed to me how my old pal Martyr Mom was actually stabbing me in the back (and in the stomach, head, face, neck, and anywhere else I experienced chronic pain or numbness). Plowing forward in service to my family without refueling, suppressing my own emotions in order to make others happy, and misunderstanding what it really meant to be loved for who I am in Christ—not what I do *for* Christ—was generating an underlying stress disorder that manifested as physical illness.

Martyr Mom was literally making me sick.

*"Do you not know that your bodies are temples of the Holy Spirit, who is in you, whom you have received from God? You are not your own; you were bought at a price. Therefore honor God with your bodies" (1 Corinthians 6:19–20).*

Since God not only owns us—heart, soul, mind, and body—but also lives within us, we owe it to Him to invest wisely in His property. Martyr Mom tries to squeeze every last drop of sacrificial blood from the temple in the name of holiness and devotion. She'll tell you it's selfish to take time for yourself, to relax and refresh, to socialize, exercise, beautify, or rest. But she's wrong. It took me not just one (duh!) but *two* ER visits to figure that out. Do you see how Martyr Mom can delude a woman's senses? Do not let her destroy God's temple. Protect it.

Maybe that means escaping to the gym a few times a week, clearing your head at a coffee shop with a friend, or taking the kids to a babysitter so you can go to the doctor or the dentist or a massage therapist. Maybe it means allocating some dollars in the budget for new jeans or shoes or haircuts—for you, not just the kids. For me, protecting God's temple means treating myself to a daily cocktail of expensive vitamins and an occasional matcha latte. Self-care is not selfish. It's an act of obedience.

*Keeping your body in shape is a spiritual discipline. It's not just about losing a few pounds, wanting to live longer, or trying to look nicer. God created your body, Jesus died for it, the Holy Spirit lives in it, your body is connected to Christ, and it's going to be resurrected one day. When it is, God's going to hold you accountable for how you managed what he gave you. —Pastor Rick Warren*[1]

## THE TRUTH ABOUT MOMMY GUILT

Many of us feel guilty for taking care of ourselves. Or perhaps after reading about Martyr Mom's tricks, you suddenly feel guilty for *not* taking care of yourself. Either way, guilt is a staple tool in Martyr Mom's belt. Due to the denial issues we explored earlier, she would have you believe that a holy woman is not supposed to struggle. Therefore, when the villains tempt us to feel grouchy, fearful, discontent, distracted, and exhausted, Martyr Mom compounds the trouble by convincing us to also feel *guilty*—for being grouchy, fearful, discontent, distracted, and exhausted.

How can a mom win?

*Consider it pure joy, my brothers and sisters, whenever you face trials of many kinds, because you know that the testing of your faith produces perseverance. Let perseverance finish its work so that you may be mature and complete, not lacking anything. (James 1:2–4)*

I used to read those verses and focus on "pure joy." Seriously? Isn't it bad enough I'm forced to face my villains—now I'm supposed to be happy about it, too? No, I realize now the Bible doesn't say that, exactly. The trial itself may not be pleasant. Trials, by definition, generally aren't. But the outcome is. Because when we have faith in Christ, God's Word says we can *know* for sure that these battles—the testing of our faith—are producing something good in us called *perseverance*. And perseverance is more than a silver lining. It's the whole point of the trial.

The Greek word for "produce" here is *katergazetai*, which means to "bring about as a result" or to "labor toward." It's not instantaneous; it's a time-consuming process. We shouldn't feel guilty about undergoing that process, because God is using it to grow us. He even tells us to "let perseverance finish its work," which further affirms we're not supposed to avoid the trial but *lean into it*.

Compare this concept to exercise. After thirty push-ups, forty burpees, and a couple sixty-second planks, I am not enjoying my aerobics class too much. It's painful! But over time, that pain produces a healthier body. So I endure and appreciate exercise for the sake of results.

Just as aerobics produce physical muscle, our trials produce spiritual muscle. We can choose to rejoice in knowing that our battles against the dirty villains are making us stronger, wiser, maturer, and complete, lacking nothing.

## GUILT VS. SHAME

When battling our villains, it's important to distinguish the difference between *guilt* and *shame*. Guilt can actually be healthy if it comes from the Holy Spirit, convicting us of thoughts or behaviors that are not aligned with God's guidance. For example, if I swipe a tube of lipstick from Walgreens, I am guilty of breaking one of God's commands: *"You shall not steal"* (Exodus 20:15). In this case, guilt is not necessarily a *feeling* but an *awareness* of having done something wrong, which will ideally prompt me to confess, return the lipstick, and ask God for forgiveness. Then He lavishes it willingly.

*"If we confess our sins, he is faithful and just and will forgive us our sins and purify us from all unrighteousness" (1 John 1:9).*

What if I have no remorse about stealing? Does that release me from my guilt? Of course not. My feelings (or lack thereof) do not change the fact that I broke God's rule. Therefore, it is possible to *be* guilty without *feeling* guilty. And guilt without remorse is dangerous because it hinders our relationship with God.

*"God detests the prayers of a person who ignores the law" (Proverbs 28:9 NLT).*

Maybe somewhere along these pages we've shared together, you've sensed God placing His finger on an area of your life that needs fixing. Embrace the conviction. Allow it to motivate you to change and grow. Holy guilt is a good thing.

*"For the kind of sorrow God wants us to experience leads us away from sin and results in salvation. There's no regret for that kind of sorrow. But worldly sorrow, which lacks repentance, results in spiritual death" (2 Corinthians 7:10 NLT).*

Shame, on the other hand, is a feeling—and it is not from God. It fixes our eyes on our failings rather than on the One who loves us in spite of them. And shame does not seek to change hearts or draw closer to the Lord; instead, it wallows in self-criticism, beats on the soul, and drowns the redeeming voice of Jesus.

*"There is now no condemnation for those who are in Christ Jesus" (Romans 8:1).*

Over time, shame has a way of festering and plaguing a woman's soul—the very thing God commands us to "keep diligently." That's why it's so important to remember grace. Martyr Mom might call you a bad mom for struggling. But God does not.

*"I sought the LORD, and he answered me; he delivered me from all my fears. Those who look to him are radiant; their faces are never covered with shame" (Psalm 34:4–5).*

## DO YOU HAVE A SAVIOR COMPLEX?

At the very heart of martyrdom is a mom's belief that her family cannot function without her. If she steps away for one moment, surely her children will run wild and dirty through the streets and then Martyr Mom will have to miss her pedicure appointment to bail them out of jail, anyway, so what's the point? If she sacrifices herself—her energy, her attention, her God-given desires—to her children, then she *and she alone* can prevent the family's sure demise.

Ah. There's a word for that kind of thinking.

Pride.

*"What you say about yourself means nothing in God's work. It's what God says about you that makes the difference"* (2 Corinthians 10:18 MSG).

Yes, sweet moms, God says you are important. We have a difficult, delicate job. But a mother is not her child's savior. Only Jesus gets that role. So trust Him enough to take care of yourself, which will make you a better caregiver for your family. Amen?

# Chapter 10

## WILL THE REAL SUPERHERO
## PLEASE SAVE THE DAY?

*You're much stronger than you think you are. Trust me.*
SUPERMAN

**Superhero:** Jesus
**Superpowers:** Love, wisdom, goodness, justice, faithfulness, mercy, grace
**Truths and Promises:** Revelation 19:11–16; Philippians 4:13; 2 Corinthians 12:9–10; Philippians 2:13; Psalm 139; Zephaniah 3:17; Luke 12:6–7; Ephesians 2:4–5; John 6:39; 1 John 3:1; Matthew 12:34; Deuteronomy 11:19; 1 Thessalonians 2:11–12; Philippians 4:8–9; Galatians 5:1; Jonah 2:8–9; Romans 1:20; James 4:8; Psalm 57:1–3; Matthew 7:7–11; Ephesians 3:16–21

———

Over the last eight chapters, we've examined our dirty villains one by one, and by now you've gleaned some practical wisdom and courage for defending yourself against their ploys. No single villain can withstand the power of God's Word when we faithfully and intentionally apply it to our lives.

Unfortunately, though, our villains rarely show up alone. Most of us battle multiple villains every day. And when they gang up on us, their combined force can feel overwhelming and, quite frankly, impossible to beat.

But are they really?

## A DAY IN THE LIFE OF A MOM

Imagine with me a typical mom-life scene. You wake up, stare at the ceiling, and make a mental promise to yourself and God. *Today I am going to be* awesome*! I love my family! I can* do this *mom deal!*

So you strap on your proverbial SuperMom cape and rise from bed, determined to be the best mom in the galaxy or at least the planet. And unlike yesterday, and the day before that, and the day before that—you get the picture—you are *really* going to do it right this time.

Just then, however, a small person patters into your room. "Mommy, I want a Popsicle. Can I have a Popsicle? For breakfast? An orange one? Wait, no, a red one. Right now? *Pleeeeeeeease? I really want a Popsicle!*"

Suddenly, the Grouch shows up out of nowhere and punches a hole through your cape.

A few minutes later, another child skips down the hall and meets you in the kitchen. "Mom, did you see the permission slip in my take-home folder? You have to sign it." So you dig through your child's backpack, find the sheet of paper, and discover her class is planning a field trip to the roller coaster park ninety miles away. *Roller coasters. Crowds. Buses without seat belts. Are you kidding me? Kids get abducted and killed at those places!*

Immediately Worry Woman sneaks up behind you and slices another gash in your SuperMom cape.

You set to work making lunches and searching for lost shoes, harping on your kids to get out the door and into the car because *school doesn't wait for us, people!* You're on a tight schedule to make that 8:30 meeting, run those errands, check a dozen e-mails, and throw dinner in the slow cooker before pick-up time. Calendar Queen shoves you behind the steering wheel and slams your cape in the door. This time it rips *and* stains in the greasy hinge.

Halfway to school you realize you forgot to draw a smiley face on your child's sandwich baggie—like that *other mom* does—and the Fence Hopper takes another nasty bite out of your cape. Darn it.

Back home, after barely flying through a crazy morning, you lay the little one down for a nap and spy a heaping pile of laundry overflowing from the hamper. You really should wash the clothes, but this might be your only quiet hour to open that book you've been eager to read. So Martyr Mom and the Maid ambush you from either side, seriously crumpling your filthy cape in the scuffle.

And that's when you hear a rattling at the door lock. Surprise! Your husband's home for lunch—and he wants a nooner. Weary Wife lights a match to your cape and sets the fool thing on fire.

By the end of the day, you're curled into a fetal position in the corner of the shower while Zombie Mommy dunks the scorched ends of your cape into a tub of Ninja Turtles bubble bath.

"Lord!" You cry out. "Look at my SuperMom cape! It's ruined! Disgusting! Beyond any hope of repair! I can't wear it anymore, God! I *can't*!"

"My dear child," God answers, "*I never asked you to.*"

## WHO'S THE REAL HERO HERE?

*Then I saw Heaven open wide—and oh! a white horse and its Rider. The Rider, named Faithful and True, judges and makes war in pure righteousness. His eyes are a blaze of fire, on his head many crowns. He has a Name inscribed that's known only to himself. He is dressed in a robe soaked with blood, and he is addressed as "Word of God." The armies of Heaven, mounted on white horses and dressed in dazzling*

*white linen, follow him. A sharp sword comes out of his*
*mouth so he can subdue the nations, then rule them with a*
*rod of iron. He treads the winepress of the raging wrath of*
*God, the Sovereign-Strong. On his robe and thigh is written,*
*KING OF KINGS, LORD OF LORDS. (Revelation 19:11–16 MSG)*

That, my fellow moms, is what a real superhero looks like.

Jesus is the mightiest warrior, the most righteous ruler, the maker of miracles, and the keeper of true superhuman power. He's not comic book fiction. Our Savior is real, readily available, and returning someday to conquer evil for good. If you have surrendered your life to Him, then you do not need to fight your dirty villains alone. The Hero fights with you. He fights *for* you.

*"I can do all things through Christ who strengthens me"* (Philippians 4:13 NKJV).

Why are we holding ourselves to a SuperMom standard? God never set that expectation. *Because there is no such thing as SuperMom.* The only "super" within you and me is God Himself. And do you know what that means? We don't have to hide from our flaws. All those triggers that conjure the villains—God says *welcome them.* Because they invite the very strength and presence of Jesus.

*But he [Jesus] said to me, "My grace is sufficient for you, for*
*my power is made perfect in weakness." Therefore I will boast*
*all the more gladly about my weaknesses, so that Christ's*
*power may rest on me. That is why, for Christ's sake,*
*I delight in weaknesses, in insults, in hardships, in persecu-*
*tions, in difficulties. For when I am weak, then I am strong.*
*(2 Corinthians 12:9–10)*

## SO NOW WHAT?

Okay, now maybe you're thinking, *Great that Jesus is my strength and all that, but practically speaking, how do I wield it?*

I'm so glad you asked. How *do* we unleash God's power in our lives? It's a question I've grappled with over the years; and the truth is, I don't have all the answers figured out. But I do know from my own experience and from walking alongside other women that God is not some long-distance, sleepy grandfather in the sky. He is alert, involved, and much closer than we imagine.

*"For God is working in you, giving you the desire and the power to do what pleases him" (Philippians 2:13 NLT).*

Let's examine five lifestyle habits that can help us tap into God's strength and wisdom as we face our dirty villains day by day.

- Believe that God loves you no matter what.
- Study God's promises and teach them to your children.
- Get rid of anything that competes with God.
- Worship the Lord as a way of life.
- Pray, pray, pray.

## BELIEVE THAT GOD LOVES YOU NO MATTER WHAT

Do you know God thinks you're fabulous? It's true. If you don't believe that, your battle against the villains is doomed from the start. Because before you can wield God's mighty power, you must first believe that *He is on your side.*

To ingest this truth deep in your heart, let's look at some supporting arguments from scripture.

### 1. God created you, and you are His masterpiece.

*"For you created my inmost being; you knit me together in my mother's womb. I praise you because I am fearfully and wonderfully made; your works are wonderful, I know that full well" (Psalm 139:13–14).*

## 2. God knows you better than you know yourself.

*"You have searched me, LORD, and you know me. You know when I sit and when I rise; you perceive my thoughts from afar. You discern my going out and my lying down; you are familiar with all my ways. Before a word is on my tongue you, LORD, know it completely. . . . All the days ordained for me were written in your book before one of them came to be" (Psalm 139:1–4, 16).*

## 3. God takes delight in you.

*"'The LORD your God is with you, the Mighty Warrior who saves. He will take great delight in you; in his love he will no longer rebuke you, but will rejoice over you with singing'" (Zephaniah 3:17).*

## 4. God watches over you. You are valuable to Him.

*"Are not five sparrows sold for two pennies? Yet not one of them is forgotten by God. Indeed, the very hairs of your head are all numbered. Don't be afraid; you are worth more than many sparrows" (Luke 12:6–7).*

## 5. God loves you enough to save you.

*"But God is so rich in mercy, and he loved us so much, that even though we were dead because of our sins, he gave us life when he raised Christ from the dead. (It is only by God's grace that you have been saved!)" (Ephesians 2:4–5 NLT).*

## 6. God will never let you go.

*"'And this is the will of him who sent me, that I shall lose none of all those he has given me, but raise them up at the last day'" (John 6:39).*

Understand that God's love for you is not dependent on what you do. It's not measured by how your kids behave or what advanced grade level they're reading. Your value is not even determined by the number of hugs and kisses and Pinterest-perfect cupcakes you shower on your family in a given day or a year.

Your value is set by God—long before you became a mom. Long before sleepless nights and diaper runs and softball tournaments stripped your energy and your glamour and caused you to question your worth.

God loves you for *who you are*. We get this: we're moms. We have an inbred love for our children that persists even when they misbehave or drive us nuts. And if we, flawed mortals that we are, can hold such deep affection for our sons and daughters in spite of their failings, imagine how much more a holy, impeccable Creator God can love us, His own children.

*"See what great love the Father has lavished on us, that we should be called children of God! And that is what we are!" (1 John 3:1).*

## STUDY GOD'S PROMISES AND TEACH THEM TO YOUR CHILDREN

I know. You don't need another lecture on how you're supposed to read your Bible every day. You've heard it a hundred times before, and you probably already feel guilty for falling behind on this cardinal "to-do" of Christian womanhood.

Fair enough. I won't tell you to read your Bible. Instead, I'll tell you a story.

One day my younger daughter, age four at the time, came running into the kitchen where I stood chopping lettuce for dinner. "Mom!" She looked at me, wide-eyed and breathless. "We need those Band-Aids!"

"We need what?" I set down the knife and crinkled my eyebrows.

"Those Band-Aids! On the TV! They're waterproof, Mom. Waterproof!"

"Oh." I nodded and resumed chopping. "I see. You heard about these Band-Aids on TV, huh?"

"Yes! We *need* them. Protection from germs, water, and dirt. Always on the go!"

Wonderful.

In our house, my husband and I limit television to channels with kid-safe commercials, but lately I'm skeptical there is such a thing. My children can hear a message once and believe it's true. Worse, they can recite it word for word and remember it for months. I've been told we must buy spill-proof snack cups, a Shark steam cleaner, something called Teddy Tanks, and—my personal favorite—a home waxing kit "because then you don't have to shave your legs, Mom! Less time in the shower, and smoother, silkier legs! You *need* that!"

All this leads me to wonder—am I just like my kids?

I mean, whatever goes in my head eventually comes out my mouth, too, right? Jesus says, *"For the mouth speaks what the heart is full of" (Matthew 12:34).* In the case of television, my children's hearts and minds get filled with commercial junk food. It does nothing to nourish their growing character. Likewise, filling my own inner spaces with anything outside of God's Word can risk not just my soul's condition but also my ability to guide others—namely, my children.

That's why the apostle Paul urges us: *"Finally, brothers and sisters, whatever is true, whatever is noble, whatever is right, whatever is pure, whatever is lovely, whatever is admirable—if anything is excellent or praiseworthy—think about such things" (Philippians 4:8).*

The more we devour God's words, the better we'll know Him and what He wants for our lives, and the more wisdom we'll have to share with our kids. Deuteronomy 11:19 says, *"Teach [God's words] to your children, talking about them when you sit at home and when you walk along the road, when you lie down and when you get up."* In other words, make God and His commands part of your everyday lifestyle. Practice what you preach.

Connect Bible verses to family rules and teachable moments. Offer mercy for mistakes, and beg forgiveness when the mistakes are yours. Encourage your kids to pray with you about anything and everything, from stuffy noses to missing library books to the car breaking down. And understand it is *our* job as parents to guide our children, no one else's. Sunday school and church programs can be wonderful supplements, but they're just that—supplements. We parents are to be the primary guides in our kids' journey toward the Lord.

*"For you know that we dealt with each of you as a father deals with his own children, encouraging, comforting, and urging you to live lives worthy of God, who calls you into his kingdom and glory"* (1 Thessalonians 2:11–12).

A woman deeply rooted in God's Word has power to fight a crowd of villains and to equip her children for their own daily battles. So I'm not telling you what to do. The choice is yours. Do you want garbage in, garbage out—or truth in, truth out?

*"Whatever you have learned or received or heard from me, or seen in me—put it into practice. And the God of peace will be with you"* (Philippians 4:9).

## GET RID OF ANYTHING THAT COMPETES WITH GOD

Remember when I told you I made a personal decision to shut down my laptop whenever my kids were home and awake? On the surface it was a practical attempt at creating a boundary between working from home and *living at home*. My family benefited from the effort for a season, and so did I—but not just because it made me more available as a wife and mom. Truth is, that experience was my rehab.

I first confronted my computer addiction a couple years ago when we went on a family vacation to Disney World. Before we left for the airport, I decided last-minute to leave my iPad at home. At the time I didn't own a smartphone, and there was no room for my laptop in anybody's backpack. So I spent a week in Orlando irreversibly unplugged.

To my great surprise, I loved it.

In the beginning, I expected a few heart palpitations, some nervous twitches or dry sweats, you know, from the sudden withdrawal. But can you believe it? As soon as we landed in Florida, I got so absorbed in vacation mode that I completely forgot about my e-mail. I shoved it to some remote corner of my brain, where deadlines and duties await, and I engaged fully with my family, my blessings. We laughed. We held hands. We built memories to last a lifetime. And none of it was distracted by the pull of the outside world.

On a normal day, I'm shamefully connected. I check messages constantly, lured by the nagging pressure to communicate—with clients, church, friends, family. I'm an author and a blogger, after all. Social media is part of the job. But is it possible to take it too far?

Like when I used to flip open my laptop first thing in the morning—before I prayed for God's blessings on the day or made my hungry daughters their breakfast.

Or when nap time afforded a quiet hour, and I reached for my iPad instead of my Bible.

Or when my girls pleaded, "Mom, let's play a game!" and I replied with those infamous words, "Just a minute!" while I stuck my nose in Gmail—again.

It took a week of sunny freedom to discover I'd been enslaved. And anything that enslaves us is not God's design.

*"It is for freedom that Christ has set us free. Stand firm, then, and do not let yourselves be burdened again by a yoke of slavery"* (Galatians 5:1).

For you, maybe it's texting, Facebook, Pinterest, or TV.

Maybe it's a hobby or your social life or a Candy Crush obsession. Whether you're a workaholic or a shopaholic or any "aholic" in between, if anything in your life competes with faith and family for your affection and attention, do what you must to subdue it beneath the throne of God.

Will it be easy? Of course not—nor is it a one-time deal. Just like we clean our house today and tomorrow it fills with clutter, our souls have a way of collecting junk. We need to declutter on a regular basis. Keep a close eye on your idols, those things competing against God for your attention. Sweep them away; don't let the dust pile up. Because if you want to maximize the Lord's power against your dirty villains, you must not let anyone or anything stand in His way.

*"Those who cling to worthless idols turn away from God's love for them. But I, with shouts of grateful praise, will sacrifice to you. What I have vowed I will make good. I will say, 'Salvation comes from the* LORD'*" (Jonah 2:8–9).*

## WORSHIP AS A WAY OF LIFE

Another key to experiencing God's power is to open your eyes and look for it. It's everywhere.

*"For since the creation of the world God's invisible qualities—his eternal power and divine nature—have been clearly seen, being understood from what has been made, so that people are without excuse"* (Romans 1:20).

I often point out the sunset to my kids. "Girls, look at the beautiful picture God painted for us in the sky tonight! Isn't He the best artist ever?"

"Yeah, Mom, look! It's purple and orange and red!"

"And, girls, check out this leaf from our tree. I wonder how God made it so smooth and green."

"Momma, look, I found a rock! Did God make rocks?"

Have you ever had those conversations with your kids? These aren't just nature lessons. When we admire creation because of the Creator, we're entering a moment of worship. We're drawing closer to the Lord who made everything and witnessing proof of His existence.

We can worship God through music, art, dancing, prayer, and many other vehicles, but those are all just outward expressions. Worship itself is a state of the heart. It doesn't require a beautiful singing voice or poetic personality. Worship is a lifestyle of acknowledging and responding to God's holiness, adoring Him and thanking Him for who He is and what He's done. God doesn't have to give us anything in return, but like a generous and loving Father, He rewards us for our worship—by giving us more of Himself.

*"Come near to God and he will come near to you" (James 4:8).*

You want to plug into God's tremendous power? Make worship your way of life. Not only will it strengthen you against the villains; it can prevent them from tackling you in the first place.

> *Have mercy on me, my God, have mercy on me, for in you I take refuge. I will take refuge in the shadow of your wings until the disaster has passed. I cry out to God Most High, to God, who vindicates me. He sends from heaven and saves me, rebuking those who hotly pursue me—God sends forth his love and his faithfulness. (Psalm 57:1–3)*

## PRAY, PRAY, PRAY

Throughout this book we've talked a lot about prayer. It's the ticket to quelling most villainous situations. But what is prayer, exactly? And why does it help?

At its core, prayer is simply conversation with God. Think of it like this: when your children wake up each day, you say good morning. You might ask them how they slept. They tell you about their silly dreams; you discuss what to eat for breakfast. You chatter about friends or school or which playground to visit. Even if your kids aren't old enough to talk, moms still "converse" in baby gibberish. You look forward to the day when those sweet cheeks form real sentences in return.

On the other hand, if you have older kids in the withdrawn, silent phase, then you know how maddening it can be when someone you love and want desperately to connect with *won't* talk to you. You long for those heart-to-hearts that help you understand what's happening in your child's world.

Prayer is kind of like that—with God as the parent. Just as your close relationship with your children involves daily communication, God also wants to hear from you day by day and hour by hour. He wants you to share what's going on in your heart. Even though, of course, He already knows, it means more coming from you. Because when you talk openly with God, you demonstrate your love and dependence on Him. And He delights in answering your prayers.

> *"Ask and it will be given to you; seek and you will find; knock and the door will be opened to you. For everyone who asks receives; the one who seeks finds; and to the one who knocks, the door will be opened. Which of you, if your son asks for bread, will give him a stone? Or if he asks for a fish, will give him a snake? If you, then, though you are evil, know how to give good gifts to your children, how much more will your Father in heaven give good gifts to those who ask him!" (Matthew 7:7–11)*

In this passage, the Greek words for "ask," "seek," and "knock" are all written in the present tense, which suggests we don't just ask/

seek/knock once and get what we ordered. Prayer is ongoing and persistent. We are to ask *continually*, seek God *daily*, and knock *again and again and again*. God will answer every time—through scripture, wise counselors, circumstances, or a personal sense of conviction—although His answer may not be what we expect. Why? Because, as the passage says, God gives only *good gifts*. And sometimes what we want for ourselves or others is not actually good according to God's all-knowing plan.

So keep praying and trusting God. Eventually, the more you seek Him, the better you'll know Him. The better you know Him, the better you'll understand what He wants for you. And your power to fight the villains will increase along with your faith.

> *I pray that out of his glorious riches he may* **strengthen you with power** *through his Spirit in your inner being, so that Christ may dwell in your hearts through faith. And I pray that you, being rooted and established in love,* **may have power***, together with all the saints, to grasp how wide and long and high and deep is the love of Christ, and to know this love that surpasses knowledge—that you may be filled to the measure of all the fullness of God. Now to him who is able to do immeasurably more than all we ask or imagine, according to* **his power that is at work within us***, to him be glory in the church and in Christ Jesus throughout all generations, for ever and ever! Amen. (Ephesians 3:16–21, emphasis added)*

# Chapter 11

## RELEASE THE BEAUTIFUL MOM INSIDE

*The door is more than it appears. It separates who you are from who
you can be. You do not have to walk through it. . .you can run.*
FRANKLIN RICHARDS (OF THE FANTASTIC FOUR)

My girls love Tinker Bell movies. We've watched all of them
multiple times, to the point where even my husband has
half the dialogue memorized. My favorite is the one where Tinker Bell first arrives in Pixie Hollow and gets assigned her trade
of tinkering. Have you seen it? According to Disney lore, fairies
are born from a baby's first laugh. So the movie depicts a giggling
infant burping up this magical wind that carries a dandelion
seedling over human fields and forests until it drops gently in the
heart of fairyland. As the seed illuminates, we see a full-grown
Tink emerge, perhaps a bit naive, yet ready to strike a hammer
and learn her life's craft.

God could have created us that way if He'd wanted to—
fully formed, adult size, speaking in intelligible sentences from
the very first day. He did it for Adam, after all, fashioning the
father of all men from dust and then Eve from Adam's rib. It's
not like this was difficult for God because, well, He's *God*, and
He can do anything. Why not just keep whipping up new grown
people to populate the planet?

Yet God chose procreation—a process involving humans,
a man and woman joining together to generate new life inside
the mother's womb, where little by little a person is formed then
pushed into the world—tiny, clueless, and wholly dependent.
On us. The parents. We are responsible to feed and nurture, teach

and train, love and guide God's children into adulthood, where someday they'll generate their own tiny people and the cycle begins again.

Why?

God doesn't *need* us. He can create people anytime and any way He likes. And He's far better at parenting than we are. So what's the point of motherhood?

Could it be that God *wants* us? That the journey of raising a child is not just for the child's benefit but ours as well? Yes, we know motherhood grows us, challenges and chisels us. It is God's tool for shaping our deepest character and drawing us, desperate, to Him.

But it goes beyond that. We're talking about *God* here. He loves to shower His children with blessings. Do you think maybe, just maybe, God granted us the job of parenting so that we, too, could experience a glimpse of the great love He feels for us, His own children?

What if parenting was created *for our enjoyment*?

*"Children are a gift from the LORD; they are a reward from him"* *(Psalm 127:3 NLT).*

The dirty villains bind and gag us, prohibiting us from enjoying motherhood the way God intended. But we know how to conquer them now. We've spent the last ten chapters discovering how to become equipped and empowered. Sure, we may still stumble in battle at times. Nobody's perfect. But, with God, we have already won the war.

We are free.

Free to release the beautiful mom inside—the woman who wants not only to nurture and teach her children but also to embrace them, delight in them, throw back her head and laugh with heavenly abandon.

Can you feel her stirring inside? It's time to let her out, moms.

And this is how we're going to do it.

- ✓ Transcend the ordinary.
- ✓ Stop wishing ahead.
- ✓ Be the fun family.
- ✓ Find an accountability partner.
- ✓ Make their memories sweet.

## TRANSCEND THE ORDINARY

Confession. Once upon a time, I wanted to be a rock star. I'm not talking about a child's pipe dream here—this was a real, adult ambition of mine for many years. I earned a college degree in contemporary music and pursued some singer/songwriter goals before I met and married my husband and settled into domestic life.

What about you? What were your dreams before kids?

I hear a lot of women, especially stay-at-home moms, struggle to define themselves according to their accomplishments or "lack" thereof. As if this child-rearing, laundry-sorting, jelly-spreading life—for which we traded all our worldly potential—is nowhere near as important as drilling wells in Africa, running a boardroom, or winning a Grammy.

We wrestle with the monotony of it all. The homework, the potty training, the vacuuming and carpooling—it's just so *dull* and *unglamorous*.

And yet ordinary moments have extraordinary value in God's eyes. He has never been as concerned with our performance as He is with our hearts. Do you have a heart to follow Jesus no matter your circumstances? No matter the audience? Parenting affords multiple opportunities day after day to do God's work. It's as simple as turning an ordinary moment into a teachable one.

On the drive to school one day, down the same route across town that my daughters and I have traveled for years, a truck swerved into our lane. I reacted quickly and avoided harm, praise God. But then the other driver flipped us off, as if the whole thing had been my fault.

"What was that signal that guy just made, Mom?" My daughters are beautifully innocent. Thankfully the gentle reply from my mouth did not betray the thoughts in my head.

"Nothing you need to worry about, my love." *Seriously, dude? You're the one who almost ran into* me*!* "It just means he is angry and unkind." *What is* wrong *with people these days?*

I caught my daughters' eyes in the rearview mirror and exhaled a puff of air from my nose. Immediately I saw God handing me an opportunity—so I took it.

"Girls," I declared, "we need to pray for him."

"Mom!" My preschooler gasped, her eyes wide with a fresh idea. "We can tell him about how Jesus died for his sins! He can be white as snow!"

And that, fellow moms, is an ordinary moment turned extraordinary.

Someday, when I get to heaven and stand in awe of my Redeemer, I don't think He will ask me why I never wrote a top-ten radio hit. I doubt He will ask about my quantity of Twitter followers or my job title or how many times I made the cover of my college alumni magazine.

Instead, these are the questions I'm preparing to answer: Did I love well? Forgive much? Did I share Jesus with other people and encourage my children to follow Him?

Did I obey when no one else was looking?

I believe God did choose you and me for greatness. You're a *great* mom. I'm a *great* wife. We're all a *great* work in progress, because our God is great, and we are His.

## STOP WISHING AHEAD

One afternoon midsummer before my older daughter started kindergarten, I ran to Walmart for half-price sparklers and hot dog buns. But when I got there, I was shocked to discover the picnic aisle had been replaced overnight with shelves upon shelves of school supplies.

For the love of flip-flops, it was only July 5! Summer in Wisconsin had barely hit its stride. I got choked up just thinking about back-to-school season, still nearly two months away. First child, first experience with full-time absence from home, Monday through Friday, September through May. Suddenly, I wanted to hold my daughter ransom, splashing through the sprinkler and slurping Popsicles like tomorrow would never come.

I hadn't always felt that way. There was a time when I wished ahead, longed for my girls to grow, to get past a rough stage, to sleep—oh glorious sleep! I reached toward the promise of easier days, and in so doing, I missed living the day I was given.

*"This is the day the LORD has made. We will rejoice and be glad in it"* (Psalm 118:24 NLT).

Do you ever add words to that verse? *Sure, Lord, I'll rejoice and be glad—as soon as the baby is sleeping through the night.*

*After those teeth poke through.*

*When she can hold her own spoon.*

*Ride her own bike.*

*Drive herself to basketball practice.*

*And you'd better believe I'll rejoice when these teenage eye rolls are a thing of the past.*

Then soon enough, they are. Along with eighteen years of beautiful childhood, which we'll never get back. I want to learn the art of living in the moment before it's too late, don't you? Before my girls wave good-bye from a college parking lot—at their sappy mother whose heart will burst into a sobbing mess as soon as our empty minivan turns the corner.

*This* is the day the Lord has made—yes, even this one. So I will rejoice and be glad in it.

*All of it.*

The toddlers and the tantrums, the math homework and milk spills, the bickering and the begging and the middle school drama. Let's take it all as it comes, moms. It's time we fight to find something to love in every stage. Then instead of wishing life away, we'll discover we're finally living it to the fullest.

## BE THE FUN FAMILY

I have this recurring nightmare in which my children are sixteen years old and they escape to a friend's house every weekend to eat pizza, sing karaoke, and play laser tag while my husband and I sit at home with our bifocals on, sipping Metamucil and reading bargain biographies. We, the wise parents, are so boring and grumpy that our children want desperately to hang out with anybody who is not us. So hubby and I spend their teen years in a state of pseudo–empty nesting before our time. *Kids these days. Humph.*

Whoa—wait a second! *Wake up!* If I have anything to say about it (and I do), my children will not grow up assuming the fun is always found somewhere else. I want them to *want* to hang out with their dad and me so we can remain their primary influence and hopefully witness to their friends in the process. As parents, we *can* establish home as the favorite place—where fun, affection, and laughter are a normal part of family life. Let's focus on three practical tips to accomplish this.

*Be spontaneous.* Step outside the usual routine every once in a while and infuse some excitement into an otherwise ordinary day. Surprise the kids with an ice cream run at bedtime. Jump in the car and go playground hopping. Book a last-minute overnight at a waterpark hotel. Eat dessert first. Yes, you're busy and you have your adult agenda, but your children will adore you for busting out of it every once in a while.

*Act like a kid.* If you prefer a wine bar over Bozo's Pizza Arcade, you're not alone. But kids would rather sip root beer; and admit it, you're a closet skee ball fan. So try entering your child's world and see how it strengthens your family bond. Blow bubbles, build forts, go roller skating, play video games and Monopoly and air guitar. Quality time with your children is a great excuse to act like a kid again. Heck, it's one of the perks of parenting.

*Model acceptance.* It's no fun living in a house where you don't measure up. Accepting your kids for who they are and nurturing their God-given potential will help establish an environment of security—a place where they know they're loved, no matter what. This might require a perspective change on your part. I call it *redefining a child's "bad" qualities.*

For example, is your kid bossy? Those are leadership skills. Hypersensitive? Call it compassionate and caring.

Rowdy = energetic, brave
Shy = discerning, introspective
Distracted = creative
Naughty = passionate, independent thinker

Get the picture? Whatever the villains interpret as evil, God can transform for good. And what a privilege we have to share in His work.

## FIND AN ACCOUNTABILITY PARTNER
Among my greatest blessings in life has been a wonderful network of Christian women friends. I realize these are not a given

for every mom, as good friends can be hard to find. If that's the case for you, then I encourage you to pray for God to bring you Christian sisters who will walk alongside you and remind you who you are in Christ.

The book of Proverbs tells us, *"Whoever walks with the wise becomes wise" (Proverbs 13:20 ESV)* and *"As iron sharpens iron, so one person sharpens another" (Proverbs 27:17).* If possible, identify a godly friend who is willing to partner with you in your daily battles. Check in with each other regularly. Share honest struggles without judgment. Pray for one another and hold each other accountable to God's truths.

An accountability partner will "sharpen" you by gently calling you on the carpet when you're blind to your own faltering, and you can do the same for her. She can listen to your heartache and help you discern the voice of God. She can encourage your victories and remind you why you're fighting in the first place.

We weren't meant to face the villains alone. Motherhood does not have to be you against the world. With an accountability partner, your team can consist of you, your friend, and Christ.

*"A person standing alone can be attacked and defeated, but two can stand back-to-back and conquer. Three are even better, for a triple-braided cord is not easily broken" (Ecclesiastes 4:12 NLT).*

## WE ARE THE MEMORY MAKERS

Well, sweet mom, I've enjoyed spending this time with you. It feels like we've become kindred spirits now, you and me. I've shared my struggles and lessons learned, maybe you've underlined a sentence or two that encouraged you through your own struggles, and together we are stronger moms for having stood this fight together. I appreciate you. I'm cheering for you.

And now I want to leave you with one final story.

Years ago, when my daughters were babies, they had a blue

bouncy seat. I used to strap them in it when I took a shower, folded laundry, or chopped vegetables for dinner. As they grew older, the seat converted to a rocking chair. I hold vivid memories of my firstborn kicking back in that chair with a stack of board books on the floor beside her, turning page after page of *Brown Bear* and *The Very Hungry Caterpillar.*

She loved that chair.

Which is why I was kind of surprised when she asked me one day, "Mom, did my sister have a bouncy seat when she was little?"

"Yes, sweetheart." I scrunched my eyebrows. "You both did."

"What color was it?"

"Blue. Don't you remember?"

"No."

Hmm. Of course, she was seven years old at the time of questioning, so she hadn't seen the seat in a couple years at least, since we donated it beyond our household. But still, my heart sank a little because I realized that a memory so deeply ingrained in my mind was blank in hers.

And it dawned on me—there must be others. How many memories do I hold dear that my children do not share? Of course they don't remember their own baby days. They might only vaguely recall toddlerhood. In a few years, they may not remember today.

Ouch. Day after day, my daughters and I are shaping the puzzle pieces of their childhood, yet they will never assemble the full picture the way I can. It seems like somebody gets cheated in this deal, right? Either my kids—because they won't comprehend their younger selves the way I do. Or me—because, well, what's the point? If my girls won't recall all the mommy sweat I invest in them—the lunch box notes, the Pictionary games, the dinosaur-shaped toast—does my daily effort really matter?

Of course.

So what if our kids won't *see* it.

They will *feel* it.

And they will *know* it.

These memories, which to me construct the whole of my experience as a parent, are to my children not so much mental images as a general understanding of what it means to be loved. To feel secure. Special. Cherished.

I see a pony ride at Disney World. They will remember how their parents carved time and attention and desired to bring them joy.

I see a monkey-face chocolate birthday cake with grandparents seated around the table. My kids will remember how family was a priority and birthdays were marked as blessings from God.

I see a growing girl weaving friendship bracelets and rolling lumpy fondant on the kitchen counter. She will remember how her mother encouraged creativity, affirmed her interests, and granted freedom to make mistakes.

What about you? What do you see? All these memories we hold close, whether precious or ordinary, orchestrated or unplanned—they all have one thing in common...

They make an impact.

*"But from everlasting to everlasting the LORD's love is with those who fear him, and his righteousness with their children's children—with those who keep his covenant and remember to obey his precepts"* (Psalm 103:17–18).

Ten or twenty years from now, our children may not recall the details. But they will possess the virtues we poured into them along the way. They'll know without a doubt how we loved them, how we prayed for them, and how we purposed to conquer our villains not just for our own sake but for theirs as well. And, God willing, they will remember and share our love for Jesus—thanks to all those years we showed them how to love Jesus, too.

"Mom, are you sure the chair was blue?" Back to our bouncy seat conversation, my seven-year-old cocked her head toward me. "I thought my sister had a yellow one."

Huh? I rewound a few years. Oh yeah. . .

"You're right, lovey." I nodded slowly. "Your seat was blue. Hers was yellow. We bought a new bouncy chair for your sister because you were still using yours when she was born. You are absolutely right. How did I forget that?"

My daughter giggled. "It's okay, Mom. Lucky for you, I have a good memory."

*Lucky me.*

I get to stock that memory with faith, hope, and love.

Because I'm a mom; therefore, I matter.

*And so do you.*

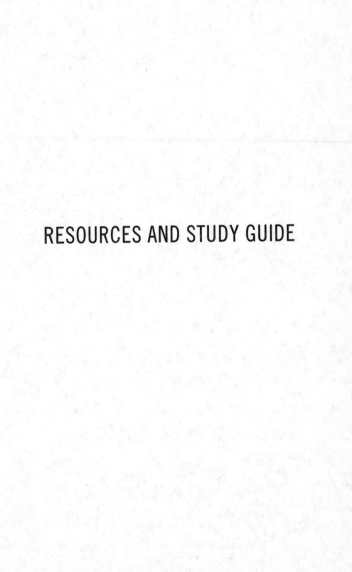

RESOURCES AND STUDY GUIDE

# A NOTE TO SINGLE MOMS

Can I give you a hug? You amazing ladies have seen some hard times and heartache, and I sincerely hope this book will help you find the encouragement and sanity you need to get up another day and do it all over again. Portions of this book, particularly "Allow Dad to Be Dad" in chapter 3 as well as most of chapter 8, are geared primarily toward married moms with a coparent in the home. If your situation involves a father who is absent, negligent, or abusive, I understand some of these words will not be relevant to your life right now. Please glean what wisdom is applicable to your situation, graciously disregard that which cannot apply to your household due to personal circumstances, and continue following God's leading for your child's well-being. Blessings to you, sweet momma!

# Chapter 1: Discussion Questions

1.  Think back to your first pregnancy or adoption. What did you think motherhood would be like? How does that compare to your actual experience?

2.  How has God used parenting to build your character?

3.  Have you ever experienced a challenge in parenting that caused you to question your abilities or worth as a mom? How did this make you feel? Now consider how you would encourage another woman coping with the same challenge.

4.  Read 2 Corinthians 1:3–4. What does this tell you about the "silver lining" of our struggles? Why is it important to console others experiencing similar trials?

5.  Is it difficult for you to open up to other women about your parenting challenges? Why? How might it help you to share your questions or concerns with supportive people?

6.  The Bible is filled with "one another" verses that urge us to be in community with others. Explore some of these and consider why God wants His people to encourage, love, and pray for one another. How does this benefit us? What does it say about God? Read John 13:34–25; 1 John 4:11; James 5:16; Hebrews 3:13; Hebrews 10:24–25; Galatians 6:1–2; Colossians 3:16; John 13:14; and Galatians 5:13.

7. Is there any "evil power" listed among the dirty villains that surprised you? Which of these hits closest to home?

8. Do you believe that God loves you and wants to help you battle your villains? Read Psalm 103:11–13; 1 John 3:1; and Zephaniah 3:17.

9. Do you have a personal relationship with Jesus? If you have never prayed to receive the Holy Spirit, our source of strength and wisdom, what's keeping you from taking this step? Read Romans 5:8; John 1:12; Romans 10:9; and Ephesians 1:13–14.

10. Read Galatians 5:22–23. How does the fruit of the Spirit compare to our list of dirty villains? Can you see why we need the Holy Spirit in order to combat them?

## Application Task

If you are past the newborn stage, call a new mom to offer encouragement or tangible help. It could be as simple as reminding her she is not alone, to as helpful as delivering a hot meal or cup of coffee. If you are in the new motherhood stages yourself, reach out to a trusted friend or mentor, or find a new moms group in your area where you can make some heart-to-heart connections with women who understand what you're going through. At any stage, memorize Lamentations 3:22–23 and make it your daily reminder. *"Because of the LORD's great love we are not consumed, for his compassions never fail. They are new every morning; great is your faithfulness."*

# Chapter 2: Discussion Questions

1. Recollect the six tricks for conquering the Grouch:

   ✓ Acknowledge her presence.
   ✓ Know who your real enemy is.
   ✓ Discern age-appropriate behavior.
   ✓ Practice the Quick Switch.
   ✓ Put a little love in your voice.
   ✓ Learn to apologize.

   Which of these do you need to work on the most? Did any of them surprise you or reveal a blind spot? Choose one strategy to put into practice today, and share the results with your discussion group or a close friend.

2. Define the difference between punishing and training. Does the "age-appropriate" principle we gained in this chapter change your perspective on your child's behavior? How does this affect your approach to discipline?

3. James 1:22 says, *"Do not merely listen to the word, and so deceive yourselves. Do what it says."* What does it mean to be deceived? When we read the Bible, listen to sermons, or pray but do not actually put the Bible's words into action, how does that harm us? Read James 1:22–25 for further insight.

4. Look up 2 Timothy 3:16–17. What is the value of scripture according to these verses? How does it benefit us? Consider how you can apply this principle to your grouchy habits.

5.  Consider a time when you had a decision to face; you knew what God's Word said about the right course of action, yet you chose another path. What was the result? How could you have protected yourself from harm if you had followed God's guidelines?

6.  Read Ephesians 4:29. What constitutes "unwholesome talk"? Do your words build others up or tear them down? Do they benefit the people who are listening? How can you improve in this area?

7.  James 3:3–10 paints a sobering picture of the power of our words. Have you considered the effect your words and tone of voice may have on your children? On your spouse? Do you control your tongue or does it control you?

8.  Read Luke 6:45. What does this say about the root of our harsh words? Now examine this verse in light of Proverbs 4:23. What does it mean to "guard your heart"? What are some practical ways we can do that?

9.  Look up Proverbs 29:20. As moms, how do we "speak in haste"? What are some practical ways we can think before we speak (i.e., prevent verbal vomit)?

10. Why is it important to establish a forgiving environment in our homes? How can this make an impact on our children's spiritual growth now and in the future?

## Application Task

Choose one day this week to "put a little love in your voice." Allow no harsh, critical, or sarcastic tones to escape from your lips. Instead, frame all of your words in kindness and patience (even if it feels forced at the time!) and take note of how this affects your child's behavior, the mood of the household, and your own state of mind.

## Quick Switch Verses

Looking for the right scripture to kick-start your Quick Switch? Here are some powerful verses, packed with truth, that apply in just about any situation that triggers the Grouch. Read them. Memorize them. Use them. They are your sword and shield.

> *The wise woman builds her house, but with her own hands the foolish one tears hers down. (Proverbs 14:1)*

> *Fathers, do not embitter your children, or they will become discouraged. (Colossians 3:21)*

> *Do not let any unwholesome talk come out of your mouths, but only what is helpful for building others up according to their needs, that it may benefit those who listen. (Ephesians 4:29)*

> *A person's wisdom yields patience; it is to one's glory to overlook an offense. (Proverbs 19:11)*

> *The words of the reckless pierce like swords, but the tongue of the wise brings healing. (Proverbs 12:18)*

*A gentle answer turns away wrath, but a harsh word stirs up anger. (Proverbs 15:1)*

*Set a guard over my mouth, LORD; keep watch over the door of my lips (Psalm 141:3).*

## Chapter 3: Discussion Questions

1. How often do you tell your kids to "be careful"? What are some practical ways we can encourage a healthy balance of both caution and courage in our children?

2. The Bible is filled with verses in which God admonishes us *not* to be afraid. (For example, see Isaiah 41:10; 2 Timothy 1:7; Philippians 4:6–7; and Joshua 1:9.) Why do you think God reminds us again and again not to fall prey to fear? What does this say about our human condition? What does it say about God?

3. How does worry affect our relationship with God? With other people?

4. Think of three traits you possess that you want to pass down to your children. Next consider three traits you do *not* want your children to learn from you. What actions can you take today to begin imparting an intentional legacy?

5. Proverbs 19:21 says, *"Many are the plans in a person's heart, but it is the LORD's purpose that prevails."* What does this tell you about our attempts to control our circumstances?

6. Consider Psalm 37:4: *"Take delight in the LORD, and he will give you the desires of your heart."* What does it mean to "take delight in the LORD"? How might our desires become better aligned with God's will?

7. Do you default to making your children's decisions for them? Why? Even at a very young age, our kids can learn to choose between two options—Cheerios or Puffs, red shoes or brown, etc. What steps can you take this week toward empowering your children to make wise, age-appropriate decisions? Where might you need to learn to back off in order to encourage your kids in this area?

8. List five ways your husband's parenting style benefits your children. Make it a point this week to thank him for these assets.

9. Is there a particular desire you've been holding close, or perhaps pulling in a tug-of-war with God? Are you willing to relinquish this desire into God's hands, praying as in Matthew 26:39, not *my* will but *Your* will be done? What are the benefits of doing this?

10. Who do you trust more—yourself or God? Read Proverbs
    3:5–6. What does it mean to acknowledge or submit to God
    in "all your ways"?

## Application Task

On a sheet of paper, write a list of your top ten worries. Fold and
seal the list in an envelope. On the front of the envelope, write a
favorite verse about worry. (Not sure which to choose? Try Philippians 4:6–7; Proverbs 3:5–6; 1 Peter 5:7; Matthew 6:33–34;
Philippians 4:13; Philippians 4:19; Luke 1:37; Matthew 11:28–
30; Psalm 55:22; Jeremiah 29:11; Isaiah 41:10; or Joshua 1:9.)
For one week, whenever any of those top ten worries pops into
your head, immediately recite your chosen verse and pray for God
to help you trust Him. At the end of the week, reflect on how this
exercise made an impact on your peace of mind.

## When Worry Is Something More

I cannot neglect to acknowledge that in some cases persistent
worry might signify a deeper struggle. If you suffer from severe
anxiety, depression, or panic attacks, then you know firsthand
how the grip of worry cannot necessarily be loosened with spiritual disciplines alone. In no way is chapter 3 meant to suggest
that mental health issues are the result of lacking faith. Please be
encouraged, sweet friends, that your condition does not render
you a lesser child of God. Just as all believers may suffer from a
variety of illnesses throughout their lives, we of strong faith are
not immune to physiological anxiety disorders. If your worry is
chronic and causes debilitating symptoms such as body aches,
digestive problems, heart issues, or the inability to sleep, concen-
trate, or carry out your daily responsibilities, please see a trusted

doctor or Christian counselor for specialized care and healing. God knows your affliction. He loves you, and He walks beside you every step of the journey. *"The LORD is close to the brokenhearted and saves those who are crushed in spirit" (Psalm 34:18).*

## Chapter 4: Discussion Questions

1. In what ways do you compare yourself to others? How does this affect the way you feel about yourself?

2. Read Genesis 1:27; Psalm 139:13–14; Matthew 5:14; Ephesians 2:10; and Zephaniah 3:17. According to these verses, how does God see you?

3. Why is God's perception of you the most accurate and trustworthy definition of who you are?

4. When does your "shoulditis" flare up? What triggers it, and how can you relieve the itch?

5. Read Exodus 20:17, one of the original commandments. What does it mean to "covet"? Who is your "neighbor"?

6. Proverbs 14:30 says, "A heart at peace gives life to the body, but envy rots the bones." How are *peace* and *envy* at odds with one another?

7. What kind of message are we sending to our kids when we criticize ourselves or wish for another person's beauty, gifts, or possessions? How can we teach our children contentment by example?

8. There is a difference between godly discontentment, which is prompted by God in order to move and grow us, and worldly discontentment, which is rooted in dissatisfaction with God's plan or blessings. How can you tell which one you are experiencing?

9. Read Psalm 37. What does it mean to "take delight in the LORD" (verse 4)? How can this lead to greater contentment?

10. Do you believe God has your best interests at heart? Read Jeremiah 29:11; Proverbs 3:5–6; Proverbs 16:9; Romans 8:28; and John 3:16–17. How do these verses encourage you to trust God's plan for your life?

## Application Task

Memorize Psalm 139:14: *"I praise you because I am fearfully and wonderfully made; your works are wonderful, I know that full well."* Whenever you are tempted toward comparison or envy, recite that verse, and ask God to help you believe it.

# Chapter 5: Discussion Questions

1. Let's take an inventory. To determine the degree to which the Calendar Queen has infiltrated your lifestyle, consider the following questions:

   - ✓ How many times a day do your children see you with your nose in a computer or mobile device?
   - ✓ Do you look your children in the eyes when you talk to them?
   - ✓ Can you sit still beside your child for ten minutes without thinking about your to-do list?
   - ✓ Do your children often need to repeat their requests before you answer them (or before you even realize they were talking to you)?
   - ✓ Do you find yourself consistently running late, rushing out the door, or telling your kids to "hurry up"?

   Now read Psalm 127. What does this tell you about God's value system? How does it compare to your own?

2. The Calendar Queen holds moms hostage with a series of untruths, which, sadly, many of us don't even recognize as harmful. Which of these lies have you believed?

   - Our children are a distraction.
   - There aren't enough hours in the day.
   - Interruptions are a nuisance.
   - Busy is better.

3. Identify three long-term goals or projects you've been putting off. What urgent needs are getting in the way of addressing these less immediate (yet still important) tasks? How can you start making time for them?

4. Do you "fold your underwear"? What lesser tasks can you pluck from the Calendar Queen's grubby hands in order to prioritize the good works God prepared for you (Ephesians 2:10)?

5. How do you handle interruptions? Read Proverbs 16:9. How does that affect the way you look at unexpected changes in your plans?

6. Read Romans 12:2. In relation to the schedules we keep, what is "the pattern of this world"? How can we "renew our minds" in order to better align our priorities with God's?

7. Is it difficult for you to "be still" (Psalm 46:10)? Why or why not?

8. Make a list of your top five priorities. Now compare that to your calendar. Does your schedule reflect your priorities? Why or why not?

9. Discuss practical ways you can remain connected to Jesus (John 15:4–8), even on hectic days or during busy seasons of life.

10. Do your children ever witness you reading your Bible, praying, or sharing your faith with others? How can we encourage their faith by example?

## Application Task

Pick a day to keep track of the number of times you say "just a minute." What did you discover? Now make a deliberate effort this week to begin *granting* minutes to your children. Discuss the results with a friend or small group.

## Quick One-Liner Prayers to Start Your Day Off Right

If you're in a season of life when it's hard to grab quiet time alone with God before family duty takes over, or if your routine involves prayer and Bible study later in the day, you can still begin each morning with the Lord. Before your feet swing out from under the covers, whisper a simple one-liner prayer, committing the day to God. Here are some suggestions.

1. Lord, help me to honor You with the way I treat my family today.

2. Please, Lord, give me eyes to see my children the way You see them.

3. Lord, I have an agenda and a schedule, but please help me to embrace *Your* plans for me, whatever today may bring.

4. Lord, search me and know my anxious thoughts; see if there is any offensive way in me, and lead me in the way everlasting (Psalm 139:23–24).

5. God, please guard my heart today.

6. Love is patient, love is kind; please, God, help me to show patience and kindness to the people I love best.

7. Today will be filled with opportunities and messages from all directions; Lord, please help me to discern which ones come from You and which I should disregard.

8. Not to me, Lord, but to You be the glory; thank You for Your love and faithfulness (Psalm 115:1).

9. Father, I believe You can do more than I ask or imagine, so please help me to see You working in my life today.

10. Lord, help me to trust You today, no matter what.

# Chapter 6: Discussion Questions

1. Which end of the spectrum can you relate to better—neat freak or neglect? Why?

2. Have your standards for housekeeping changed since becoming a mom? Why or why not?

3. Whose expectations are you striving to reach regarding housework? (Yours or someone else's?) How do those expectations compare to God's priorities?

4. Does housework prevent you from enjoying your family? On the flip side, does family life prevent you from doing housework? How can you meet somewhere in the middle?

5. Do you ever feel guilty for tending to adult responsibilities when your children want to play? It's true we need to be cautious of those "just a minute" defaults, as we saw in chapter 5. However, why is it healthy to balance work and play?

6. Jesus trained His disciples to carry out God's work. Children can learn simple tasks, such as picking up toys, as early as age one or two. What can you do this week to begin training your disciples? What biblical values might you instill in them through housework (such as obedience, respect for authority, etc.)?

7.  Whether you own or rent, your home is a provision from God. Do you value it as such? How can you develop a healthy sense of appreciation for your household?


8.  Do you crave recognition for your work? Why or why not? What does it mean to work "as though you were working for the Lord rather than for people" (Colossians 3:23 NLT)?


9.  Read Romans 12:9–13. Verse by verse, discuss how these commands apply to home keeping.


10. How is housework an opportunity to be more like Jesus?

## Application Task

Let's train our eyes to see joy in the mess. Examine a typical disaster in your household (the kitchen after dinner, your child's bedroom, etc.), then name five blessings within that scene. What did you find? How does this perspective affect the way you feel about your household?

# Chapter 7: Discussion Questions

1.  What circumstances in your life cause you to lose sleep? Is your exhaustion due to factors you can't control (nighttime feedings, sick children, etc.), or are you making choices that deprive you of sleeping hours?

2.  Isaiah 40:31 says, *"Those who hope in the LORD will renew their strength."* What does it mean to hope in the Lord? In what practical ways can we place our hope in God during exhausting seasons of life?

3.  What is the craziest thing you've ever done due to mommy fatigue? Discuss with a friend or small group.

4.  Ephesians 3:20 in *The Message* says, *"God can do anything, you know—far more than you could ever imagine or guess or request in your wildest dreams! He does it not by pushing us around but by working within us, his Spirit deeply and gently within us."* What does this tell you about God's ability to energize you during times of fatigue?

5.  Consider Joy's story of the Glo Worm. Have you ever sensed God asking you to do something that made no sense at the time? How did you respond, and what was the result? Did Joy's story impact your view of how God works in our lives?

6.  When God gives you more than you can handle, what should you do?


7.  Romans 12:1 tells us to "offer your bodies as a living sacrifice." In what ways is sleep deprivation a sacrifice to God?


8.  Read Hebrews 4:15. How can Jesus empathize with our weaknesses? Do you think He also experienced the pain of fatigue?


9.  In what ways can exhaustion lead us to sin? (Think back to Zombie Mommy's pal, the Grouch on the Couch.)


10. Although certain seasons of parenting are more exhausting than others, each stage has its positive points. Name some blessings and benefits of the newborn stage and other tiring phases of motherhood.


## Application Task

Look up Isaiah 40:29; Psalm 18:31–32; and Philippians 4:13. Write these verses on sticky notes and tack them to your bathroom mirror, your car dashboard, and inside your kitchen cupboard. Whenever exhaustion threatens to break your spirit, recite these verses and pray to God for a supernatural degree of energy to get through the day.

# Chapter 8: Discussion Questions

1. God's priorities for us are (1) God first, (2) spouse second, (3) children third. Are your priorities aligned with God's? Even when children require the majority of your time and attention, how can you prioritize God and your husband above them? (Hint: It's not just a practical concern but also a heart issue. For scripture that supports the principle of God's priorities for the family, see Deuteronomy 6:5; Ephesians 5:22–33; Ephesians 6:1–3; and Proverbs 22:6.)

2. Did your relationship with your husband change when your first child was born? How? Has parenting taught you anything new about your spouse?

3. Consider the four areas in which Weary Wife affects a marriage: romance, friendship, communication, and sex. On a scale of 1 to 10 (1 = seriously lacking; 10 = no problems) how much room for improvement do you see in each of these areas? Which one strikes you most?

4. Do you date your husband? What are the obstacles to spending one-on-one time together? How can you overcome them?

5. Why is it important to maintain an intentional romance with your husband? How does this impact your family?

6. Do you treat your husband as a friend or adversary? Why do you think it's so easy to bicker with a spouse? What does God's Word say about that? (See Philippians 2:1–4; 1 Corinthians 13:4–7; James 3:3–6; Proverbs 12:18; Proverbs 20:3; Proverbs 21:19; Proverbs 21:23; Ephesians 4:29.)

7. Brainstorm with your husband a list of recreational activities you could feasibly enjoy as a couple. Why does "playing together" help you *stay* together?

8. What is your love language? Go to www.5lovelanguages .com/profile/ to take an online quiz. Ask your husband to take it, too. Discuss how you can "speak" to each other more effectively.

9. Did this chapter give you new insights into the importance of sex in marriage? What hinders you from enjoying a mutually healthy sex life with your husband?

10. Marriage is a daily recommitment. No matter what you're facing today, what small action can you take to live out your marriage vows?

## Application Task

Write a list of things you love about your husband. These can be anything from character traits to physical attributes to memories you share. Seal it in an envelope (scented with your signature perfume if you have one) and deliver it somewhere discreet—under his pillow, taped to his bathroom mirror, tucked in his briefcase, etc. Don't be disappointed if he doesn't respond the way you expect. Do this simply as a step of faith toward rekindling your connection. Then pray that God would work in your husband's heart as well as yours to make your marriage a top priority in your lives.

## Chapter 9: Discussion Questions

1. Galatians 3:26 (NLT) says, *"For you are all children of God through faith in Christ Jesus."* Why does your identity as God's child trump all other roles you play? How can you weave this identity into every aspect of your life?

2. Do you believe God loves you? Why does He want *you* to love you, too?

3. Do you find it difficult to take care of yourself? Why or why not?

4. How do you behave toward your family when you're physically or emotionally worn out?

5. Read the parable of the talents in Matthew 25:14–30. What does this tell you about God's desires for your life? What "talents" (skills, possessions, or spiritual gifts) has He given you? How are you investing them?

6. How can you be grateful and truthful at the same time, even in seasons of heartache?

7. Is there any aspect of your life right now that needs emotional healing? What prevents you from being vulnerable and honest with the Lord or with other people?

8. What triggers your mom guilt? How can you tell the difference between godly conviction and shame?

9. What activities are you considering or currently involved in beyond your role as a mom? Examine each of these according to the five practical steps we outlined: (1) pray, (2) get your husband's support, (3) set boundaries, (4) reevaluate regularly, and (5) resist the temptation to compare. Do any concerns come to light? Any confirmations?

10. What can you do on a daily or weekly basis to "keep your soul diligently"?

## Application Task

Identify your greatest self-care need right now. Are you sick? Exhausted? Stressed? Needing adult interaction or time alone? If possible, arrange to spend a few hours addressing this need by investing in your own well-being. Take a nap. See a doctor. Go to a movie. Visit a friend. Find a corner coffee shop to hide in while you read a book for fun. Pray. Whatever will refuel you so you can again "pour out" to your family, do it—and keep in mind that your husband may also need similar opportunities to refuel. Encourage one another to make these self-care investments a regular habit for the good of the whole family.

## Chapter 10: Discussion Questions

1. Describe your typical day. How many dirty villains do you face from sunup to sundown?

2. Where did we come up with the concept of SuperMom in the first place? What impossible standards have you set for yourself?

3. Why is it safe to reveal our flaws to God? Are you willing to share those same flaws with other women? Why or why not?

4. Which of the supporting scriptures regarding God's love spoke to your heart the most?

5. Why is it important to study God's Word? How are you doing in this area?

6. Take a close look at your daily habits. What do you think about? What attracts your attention and your energy? Can you identify anything that competes with God for your head and heart?

7. What does worship mean to you? When do you experience closeness with God?

8. How can you incorporate more worship into your everyday life?

9. How does prayer strengthen your relationship with God?

10. Which of the five lifestyle habits (believe God loves you, study God's Word, get rid of idols, worship, pray) do you need to work on most? What one step will you take this week to build this habit?

## Application Task

Choose a time of day to read a family devotion or pray with your children. For example, pray in the car on the way to school, discuss a daily devotion at dinnertime, or read a passage of scripture together every night before bed. Make this part of your daily routine to show your children that God is central to your everyday lives and you rely on Him for strength and guidance.

# Chapter 11: Discussion Questions

1. What prevents you from delighting in your family? Do you battle certain villains more than others?

2. Do you struggle to find value in the mundane tasks and routines of family life? Why or why not? How does your life look different from what you imagined before you had children?

3. First Samuel 16:7 says, "People look at the outward appearance, but the LORD looks at the heart." How can you apply that truth to your "unglamorous" role as a mom?

4. Think of a time you transformed an ordinary moment into an extraordinary offering to God. Did you even realize the value of your work at the time?

5. Have you been guilty of wishing ahead? List three blessings in your current stage of parenting that you will miss when they're gone.

6. Why is it important to establish home as your children's favorite place?

7. Do you have a hard time relating to your children at their level? What can you do this week to enter their world and infuse some laughter into your family time?

8. List your child's challenging qualities. Then redefine them with a positive perspective. What can you do to nurture your child's strengths for good purposes?

9. How can we benefit from godly friendships and account-ability partners? Read the "one another" verses of the Bible for insight:

- Love one another—John 13:34; 1 John 4:11; 1 Peter 4:8
- Pray for one another—James 5:16
- Encourage one another—1 Thessalonians 5:11; Hebrews 3:13; Hebrews 10:24–25
- Hold one another accountable—Galatians 6:1; Ephesians 4:15
- Carry one another's burdens—Galatians 6:2
- Teach one another—Colossians 3:16; Titus 2:3–5
- Serve one another—John 13:14; Galatians 5:13

10. What do you want your children to remember about their childhood? With God's help, you *can* instill in them an over-arching sense of love and security. Blessings, sweet mom!

## Application Task

For one week, focus each day on transforming the ordinary. Look for teachable moments and opportunities to share God with your children and other people. Keep a journal of your experiences and note related Bible verses to support your efforts. At the end of the week, talk with a close friend or accountability partner about what you learned and how your efforts impacted you and your family.

# ACKNOWLEDGMENTS

To Jesus, my hero. To your name be all the glory.

To Chad, my love, and my partner on the journey. If SuperDad were a thing, I'd vote for you.

To my chickadees. You have taught me more than I've taught you. Mom loves you infinity plus 120,000.

To my family, especially my mom. In my childhood eyes, you were Wonder Woman—whether you felt like it or not.

To Amber, my evergreen friend. Thank you for loving me through every season.

To my agent, Blythe Daniel. Thank you for believing in me. I count you among my greatest blessings.

To Kelly McIntosh, Shalyn Sattler, and the entire Barbour team. God blessed me when he placed this book in your capable hands. Thank you for bringing it to life so beautifully.

To Judy Episcopo and Heidi Scott. Thank you for your generous time and honest feedback throughout the writing process.

To my mentor moms—Cindy K., Cindi D., Tami Z., Tammy M., Debbie S., Judy E., and Mom Judy—thank you for encouraging me, investing in me, and teaching me by example what godly parenting really means. I am so grateful for each of you.

To my dear friends and all the women of Appleton Alliance Church. You ladies are medicine for my soul.

To Heidi Maranell, my co-star in the ever-unfolding God story. I wonder what he'll do next.

To Alicia Bruxvoort, a woman who knows my heart. You are a gift straight from Jesus.

To Linda Wichman, who tread the path before me. Thank you for your guidance and love.

To Wendi Kohler for opening your home and supporting me in word and deed.

To Joy, Jamie, Sarah, Alicia, and Tammy for allowing me to share your stories.

To Amanda Chavez for your inspiring design work.

To my blog readers. Thank you for inviting me into your hearts week after week. I am truly grateful for each one of you.

And to you, the woman holding this book. Thank you for pouring your daily energy into the next generation of faith-filled human beings. Your work has eternal value. God bless you!

# NOTES

**Chapter 2**

1. Brad Bushman, "Anger Management: What Works and What Doesn't," *Get Psyched!* (blog), *Psychology Today*, September 25, 2013, http://www.psychologytoday.com /blog/get-psyched/201309/anger-management-what -works-and-what-doesnt.

2. Kristen Strong, "Three Reasons Why Your Mess Makes You a Great Mama," *Chasing Blue Skies* (blog), January 21, 2014, http://chasingblueskies.net/3-reasons-why-your-mess -makes-you-a-great-mama/.

**Chapter 4**

1. Charles R. Swindoll, "Listening to Jesus beside the Sea," Insight for Living Ministries, http://www.insight.org /resources/articles/pastors/listening-to-jesus.html.

2. Charles F. Stanley, "Living above Circumstances," In Touch Ministries, March 7, 2011, http://www.crosswalk.com /devotionals/in-touch/in-touch-mar-7-2011.html.

**Chapter 5**

1. Nancy Leigh DeMoss, *Lies Women Believe and the Truth That Sets Them Free* (Chicago: Moody, 2001), 118.

**Chapter 7**

1.  Hawley E. Montgomery-Downs et al., "Normative Longitudinal Maternal Sleep: The First Four Postpartum Months," *American Journal of Obstetrics and Gynecology* 203, no. 5 (November 2010), http:/www.ajog.org /article/50002-9378(10)00837-9/abstract.

**Chapter 8**

1.  "Tips for Parents," The 5 Love Languages, http://www.5lovelanguages.com/.

2.  Juli Slattery, "Understanding Your Husband's Sexual Needs," Focus on the Family, July 20, 2010, http: //www.focusonthefamily.com/marriage/sex-and-intimacy /understanding-your-husbands-sexual-needs.

3. Ibid.

4. Ibid.

5. Ibid.

6. Ibid.

**Chapter 9**

1. Rick Warren, "Take Care of Your Body," *Daily Hope with Rick Warren* (blog), May 21, 2014, http://rickwarren.org /devotional/english/take-care-of-your-body.

# ABOUT THE AUTHOR

Becky Kopitzke is a freelance writer, speaker, singer, dreamer, potty trainer, lunch packer, snowman builder, and sidewalk chalk artist. She lives with her handsome husband and their two young daughters in northeast Wisconsin, where a pink indoor trampoline fills half the once formal living room.

Becky welcomes fellow frazzled moms to connect with her on her blog, *Time Out: Devotions for Moms* (beckykopitzke.com). There she shares weekly devotions encouraging imperfect moms to follow a grace-filled God. Becky is also a regular contributor to For the Family (forthefamily.org) and The MOM Initiative (themominitiative.com), two inspiring resources for Christian families. Beyond writing, Becky serves in women's ministry and worship arts at her regional evangelical church and volunteers often at her daughters' school. And sometimes she serves cereal for dinner.

Becky believes parenting is one of God's greatest tools for building our faith, character, and strength—and it's not always pretty. Her writing offers solidarity, encouragement, and validation for fellow imperfect moms, for the purpose of pointing our weaknesses, blessings, and victories to God.